Schema Therapy combines proven cognitive behavioral therapy techniques with elements of interpersonal, experiential, and psychodynamic therapies in order to help people with long-term mental health problems including personality disorders and chronic depression. Schema Therapy suggests that many negative cognitive conditions are based on past experiences, and therefore provides models for challenging and modifying negative thoughts and behaviors in order to provoke change.

In this book, Eshkol Rafaeli, David Bernstein and Jeffrey Young – pioneers of the Schema Therapy approach – indicate the 30 distinctive features of Schema Therapy, and how the method fits into the broader CBT spectrum.

Divided into two parts, Theoretical Points and Practical Points. This book provides a concise introduction for those new to the technique, as well as a discussion of how it differs from the other cognitive behavioral therapies for those experienced in the field.

**Eshkol Rafaeli** is a Clinical Psychologist specializing in both cognitive behavioral therapy and Schema Therapy and is Associate Professor at Bar-Ilan University, Israel.

**David P. Bernstein** is Associate Professor in the Faculty of Psychology at Maastricht University, The Netherlands.

**Jeffrey Young** is the Founder and Director of the Cognitive Therapy Centers of New York and Connecticut, and the Schema Therapy Institute in New York City.

Cognitive behavior therapy (CBT) occupies a central position in the move towards evidence-based practice and is frequently used in the clinical environment. Yet there is no one universal approach to CBT and clinicians speak of first-, second-, and even third-wave approaches.

This series provides straightforward, accessible guides to a number of CBT methods, clarifying the distinctive features of each approach. The series editor, Windy Dryden, successfully brings together experts from each discipline to summarize the 30 main aspects of their approach divided into theoretical and practical features.

*The CBT Distinctive Features Series* will be essential reading for psychotherapists, counselors, and psychologists of all orientations who want to learn more about the range of new and developing cognitive behavioral approaches.

**Titles in the series:**

*Acceptance and Commitment Therapy* by Paul E. Flaxman, J.T. Blackledge and Frank Bond

*Beck's Cognitive Therapy* by Frank Wills

*Behavioral Activation* by Jonathan Kanter, Andrew M. Busch and Laura C. Rusch

*Compassion Focused Therapy* by Paul Gilbert

*Constructivist Psychotherapy* by Robert A. Neimeyer

*Dialectical Behaviour Therapy* by Michaela A. Swales and Heidi L. Heard

*Metacognitive Therapy* by Peter Fisher and Adrian Wells

*Mindfulness-Based Cognitive Therapy* by Rebecca Crane

*Rational Emotive Behaviour Therapy* by Windy Dryden

*Schema Therapy* by Eshkol Rafaeli, David P. Bernstein and Jeffrey Young

For further information about this series please visit www.routledgementalhealth.com/cbt-distinctive-features

# Schema Therapy

## Distinctive Features

Eshkol Rafaeli,
David P. Bernstein
and Jeffrey Young

LONDON AND NEW YORK

First published 2011
by Routledge
27 Church Road, Hove, East Sussex BN3 2FA

Simultaneously published in the USA and Canada
by Routledge
270 Madison Avenue, New York, NY 10016

*Routledge is an imprint of the Taylor & Francis Group, an Informa business*



Typeset in Times by Garfield Morgan,
Swansea, West Glamorgan
Printed and bound in Great Britain by
TJ International Ltd, Padstow, Cornwall
Cover design by Sandra Heath



This publication has been produced with paper manufactured to strict environmental standards and with pulp derived from sustainable forests.

*British Library Cataloguing in Publication Data*
A catalogue record for this book is available from the British Library

*Library of Congress Cataloging in Publication Data*
Rafaeli, Eshkol, 1970–
Schema therapy : distinctive features / Eshkol Rafaeli, David P. Bernstein & Jeffrey Young.
p. ; cm.
ISBN 978-0-415-46298-3 (hbk.) – ISBN 978-0-415-46299-0 (pbk.) 1. Schema-focused cognitive therapy. I. Bernstein, David P. II. Young, Jeffrey E., 1950- III. Title.
[DNLM: 1. Cognitive Therapy–methods. 2. Mental Disorders–therapy. WM 425.5.C6 R136s 2010]
RC489.S34R34 2010
616.89'1425–dc22

2010014269

ISBN: 978-0-415-46298-3 (hbk)
ISBN: 978-0-415-46299-0 (pbk)

# Contents

# Introduction

Cognitive behavioral therapy (CBT) has developed a strong identity as an umbrella term for time-limited evidence-based treatments for Axis I disorders. Yet CBT models for addressing personality disorders and other enduring patterns of relational and emotional difficulties are gaining greater attention. One of the leading models is Schema Therapy, first introduced by Young (1990) and more recently elaborated by Young and his colleagues (Young, Klosko, & Weishaar, 2003).

Schema Therapy is an integrative approach, bringing together elements from cognitive therapy (and CBT more generally), attachment and object relations theories, and Gestalt and experiential therapies. Our aim is to present the features that distinguish Schema Therapy within the broader cognitive behavioral field. As we make clear in the ensuing chapters, there are both theoretical and practical distinctions. But some overarching distinctions are worth noting here. First, unlike more traditional CBT approaches, Schema Therapy is explicitly concerned with the development (etiology) of current symptoms, and not only with the factors that maintain them. Second, it places a great emphasis on the therapist–patient relationship, and on providing within it both a corrective emotional experience and empathic confrontation. Third, it sets a clear goal to which the therapist should aspire: helping patients understand their core emotional needs and learn ways of getting those needs met in an adaptive manner, which requires altering long-standing cognitive, emotional, relational, and behavioral patterns.

The first half of this book (Points 1–15) details the theoretical model espoused by schema therapists. This model devotes great attention to core universal emotional needs (Point 1), and argues that maladaptive schemas (Points 2 and 3) emerge when these needs are not met. It also recognizes the existence of three broad and maladaptive coping styles: surrender, avoidance, and overcompensation (presented in Point 4 and detailed in Points 5–7).

In the past 15 years, a refinement of Schema Therapy has led to the development of an additional construct, that of *modes*, which has become crucial to the work of schema therapists. We describe this concept generally (Point 8) and then pay greater attention to the main types of modes encountered in clinical work (Points 9–13). Finally, we conclude the theoretical half of the book with a discussion of the therapeutic stances central to Schema Therapy: limited reparenting and empathic confrontation (Points 14–15).

The second half of this book (Points 16–30) discusses the application of Schema Therapy. It begins, as the therapy itself does, with the assessment phase (Points 16–18) and with the culminating case conceptualization which is presented to the patient and which guides the subsequent treatment (Point 19). It then reviews the four large toolboxes that schema therapists have at their disposal, and that include relational, cognitive, emotion-focused, and behavioral techniques (Points 20–23), as well as specific ideas for working with modes (Point 24). The following points (25–27) explore the use of Schema Therapy with particular patient populations (individuals with borderline, narcissistic, and antisocial personality, as well as couples experiencing relational distress). Point 28 is devoted to the interplay between Schema Therapy (for long-standing issues) and other CBT and evidence-based treatments (for more acute Axis I disorders or symptoms). Point 29 returns to the issue of limited reparenting, this time from a practical perspective. And Point 30 highlights the importance of attending to the therapists' own schemas and coping styles, as they come in contact with their patients' needs, schemas, coping styles, and modes.

This last point highlights one more feature that distinguishes Schema Therapy, particularly when compared with other approaches for the treatment of personality disorders or long-standing relational problems: it is decidedly a compassionate and humane approach. The assumption is that everyone has needs, schemas, coping styles, and modes – they are simply more pronounced and less flexible in the patients we treat.

# Part 1

# THEORETICAL POINTS

# 1

## Universal core emotional needs

Schema Therapy begins with recognizing a set of universal emotional needs. These include the needs for safety, stability, nurturance, and acceptance, for autonomy, competence, and a sense of identity, for the freedom to express one's needs and emotions, for spontaneity and play, and for a world with realistic limits which fosters the emergence of self-control.

Everyone has emotional needs – in fact, we argue that everyone has these particular needs. Individuals may differ in the strength of particular needs – some people may have a stronger temperamental need for spontaneity and creative expression, some may be particularly wired to crave nurturance. But above and beyond these individual differences lies a universal similarity – we all, fundamentally, have some amount of all of these needs.

Emotional needs are present from childhood; indeed, most are at their strongest in childhood. For example, the need for safety or stability, though life-long, has its strongest implications the more vulnerable or helpless one is.

Psychological health is the ability to get one's needs met in an adaptive manner. The central project of children's development is to get their core needs met; the central project of effective parenting or childrearing is to help the child get these needs met; and the central project of Schema Therapy – its primary objective – is to help adults get their own needs met, even though these needs may not have been met in the past.

In addition to the core universal emotional needs, Schema Therapy recognizes the existence of needs that emerge in adulthood (for example, the need to work and the need to care for others). These needs are also important for psychological health, but they tend not to be the focus of therapy. One possibility is that when more fundamental (and earlier) emotional needs are met in an adequate manner, individuals have the capacity to handle later needs quite well.

Schema Therapy has its roots in cognitive behavioral therapy (CBT) (as we detailed in the Introduction and will return to in Point 28). But CBT does not typically address universal needs. If needs get invoked in cognitive therapy, it's in an ad-hoc manner, when a patient or a therapist identifies them. Some cognitive behavioral approaches actually disdain needs – grouping them together with "shoulds" and "oughts" – rigid constructs that are best avoided. This is one example of how Schema Therapy departs from other CBT approaches, and of how it integrates useful ideas from other orientations (in this case, emotion-focused, attachment, and dynamic approaches).

Indeed, needs have been the focus of earlier clinical theories (e.g., control/choice theory: Glasser, 1969; the hierarchy of needs: Maslow, 1962) and are gaining some prominence in more recent research in personality, social, and developmental psychology (e.g., Baumeister and Leary's (1995) need for belonging, or the broader work of self-determination theory on the universal needs for autonomy, competence, and relatedness (Deci & Ryan, 2000)).

Needs – especially those for nurturance, warmth, and security – are also central to attachment theory. Attachment theory has been a prominent approach to human development for the past half century, beginning with John Bowlby's strikingly powerful observation that phenomena observed by evolutionary ethologists (like Lorenz and Harlow) have direct implications to child development, and to human social and emotional development more generally. As decades of both human and primate research show, secure attachment early in life serves as the basis for many adaptive processes later on: with a "secure base," the child is able to develop curiosity and exploration, self-soothing and self-regulation, and ultimately the ability to form close emotional bonds.

Attachment theory and research have been major sources of influence on Schema Therapy. The ideas of Bowlby and Ainsworth (as well as of other writers from the British Object Relations School, particularly Margaret Mahler and Donald Winnicott) are one of the three legs on which Schema Therapy stands, and the one which most clearly spells out the notion of needs. (The other two legs, to which we turn in later points, are CBT and experiential/emotion-focused approaches.)

Some of the theories that speak strongly about needs (including, for example, Maslow's hierarchy model as well as attachment theory) give certain needs "privileged" status – viewing them as more basic or fundamental. For example, attachment theory assumes that if attachment security needs are not attained, other (later) needs will be impeded. Schema Therapy avoids making assumptions such as these regarding a "hierarchy" or a gradient of importance. Instead, core needs are all seen as essential and universal, especially in the lives of adults.

A final point about needs as a feature of Schema Therapy: educating patients about needs in general, and about their own unmet (as well as met) needs, can be quite a powerful intervention in its own right. Being told (as many of our patients are) that they are needy, not greedy, and that the therapy is aimed at helping them get their needs met, helps provide a non-judgmental view of the past and a focused, optimistic view of the future.

2

# Early maladaptive schema development as a consequence of unmet needs

The concept that gives Schema Therapy its name is of course the *schema*, a word of Greek origin ($\sigma\chi\eta\mu\alpha$) that refers to a pattern or an organizing framework which helps create order in a complex set of stimuli or experiences. Schemata (or as they're more commonly referred to, schemas) have a rich history in a variety of fields, including philosophy, computer science, set theory, and education, to name a few. In psychology, schemas were first introduced in the cognitive/developmental literature, and from there, made their way into cognitive therapy (Beck, 1972).

In cognitive developmental research, the concept of schemas refers to patterns imposed on reality or experience to help individuals explain it, to mediate perception, and to guide their responses. A schema is an abstract representation of the distinctive characteristics of an event, a kind of blueprint of its most salient elements. Within cognitive psychology, a schema can also be thought of as an abstract cognitive plan that serves as a guide for interpreting information and solving problems. Thus we may have a linguistic schema for understanding a sentence or a cultural schema for interpreting a myth. The term "schema" in psychology is probably most commonly associated with Piaget (e.g., 1955), who wrote in detail about schemata in different stages of childhood cognitive development, and with Bartlett (1932), who originated the use of this term and demonstrated the roles of schemata in learning new information, as well as in recalling memories.

Moving from cognitive psychology to cognitive therapy, Beck referred in his early writing (e.g., 1972) to schemata. Yet the idea that schemas, or broad organizing principles, exist in every person's life and guide the person in making sense of their own life is inherent in many approaches to therapy, cognitive or otherwise. Likewise, many theorists would agree that schemas are often formed early in life, but continue to be elaborated and developed over the lifespan. Also common to many approaches is the notion that schemas, which might have accurately captured earlier life experience, are often brought to bear in current life situations for which they are no longer applicable. In fact, that is exactly what cognitive and developmental psychologists would have predicted – that schemas would operate in a way that maintains our sense of cognitive consistency. That is how schemas function – they serve as shortcuts, bringing us quickly towards what we think is *likely* to be true and saving us the need to carefully process every detail we encounter. In some cases, schemas or shortcuts are quite efficient in helping us reach a fairly accurate grasp of the situation. But in others, they paint quick-and-dirty pictures for us that are inaccurate and distorted. In either case, they help us maintain a stable view of ourselves and our world – whether that stable view is accurate or inaccurate, adaptive or maladaptive.

Stability and predictability sound like good qualities to have, and they very well could be in some instances. For example, one kind of schema – mental scripts – helps us anticipate how one step (e.g., the main course) is going to follow another (e.g., the appetizer) so that we can handle being in an entirely new place (e.g., an unknown restaurant, even one in a foreign country where we do not speak the language) while still keeping our bearings. Even when a schema is not entirely accurate, it may, in some instances, still be harmless. For example, another kind of schema – group stereotypes – can lead us to respect a new acquaintance or to assume her to have some outstanding capacity, solely on the basis of her race, gender, country of origin, etc.

Yet some schemas – especially ones acquired as a result of toxic childhood experiences and related to the self and the interpersonal world – can be pernicious in their effects. Schemas such as these, which we label *early maladaptive schemas* are the focus of Schema Therapy, and are at the core of personality disorders, relational difficulties, and some Axis I disorders.

Young, Klosko, and Weishaar (2003) provided the following comprehensive definition of an early maladaptive schema:

- A broad, pervasive theme or pattern
- Comprised of memories, emotions, cognitions, and bodily sensations
- Regarding oneself and one's relationships with others
- Developed during childhood or adolescence
- Elaborated throughout one's lifetime, and
- Dysfunctional to a significant degree.

In other words, early maladaptive schemas are self-defeating emotional and cognitive patterns that begin early in our development and repeat throughout life. Note that according to this definition, an individual's behavior is not part of the schema itself – instead, maladaptive behaviors are thought to develop as logical responses to a schema. Thus, behaviors are driven by schemas, but are not part of schemas. Many behaviors reflect the way we cope with schemas – and we discuss them in detail when we address coping styles in Points 4–7.

Early maladaptive schemas (which we will refer to simply as schemas from now on) emerge from toxic early experiences – ones in which a young person's needs were profoundly not met. Most early needs (e.g., the need for safe and secure attachment, the need for nurturance) are present in their strongest form within a young child's nuclear family. For this reason, problems within the close family unit are usually the primary origin of early maladaptive schemas. The schemas that develop earliest and are closest to a person's core typically originate in the nuclear family. To a large extent, the dynamics of a child's family are the dynamics of that child's entire early world. When patients find themselves in adult situations that activate their early maladaptive schemas, what they usually are experiencing is a drama from their childhood, usually with a parent.

Other arenas that become increasingly important as the child matures include one's peers, extended family, school, groups in the community, and the surrounding culture. Toxic experiences in these arenas – that is, experiences in which core emotional needs go unmet – may also lead to the development of schemas. However, schemas developed at later ages are generally not as pervasive or as powerful as ones developed early on, in the close family arena. This may be because of the nature of those needs directed towards the family; it could also be because of the longer duration of contact between a child and their family of origin (compared with most peer, school, or neighborhood contacts).

We have observed four types of early life experiences that foster the acquisition of schemas. The first is toxic frustration of needs. This occurs when the child experiences "too little of a good thing," and acquires schemas that reflect deficits in the early environment. The child's environment is missing something important, such as stability, understanding, or love – and that lack becomes a permanent presence in the child's mind.

A second type of early life experience that engenders schemas is traumatization. Here, the child is harmed or victimized, and develops schemas that reflect the presence of danger, pain, or threat. The core emotional need for safety is unfulfilled; worse, it is directly challenged, often leading to schemas marked by mistrust, hypervigilance, anxiety, and hopelessness.

In a third type of experience, the child experiences "too much of a good thing": the parents provide the child with too much of something that, in moderation, is healthy for a child. With schemas of this sort, the child is almost never mistreated, but instead, is coddled or indulged. The child's core emotional needs for autonomy or realistic limits are not met. Thus, parents may be overly involved in the life of a child, may overprotect a child, or may give a child an excessive degree of freedom and autonomy, without any limits.

The fourth type of life experience that creates schemas is selective internalization or identification with significant others. The child selectively identifies with, and internalizes, the thoughts, feelings, experiences, and behaviors of an influential adult, usually a parent. One way to think of this process is as modeling – parents or other adults modeling for the young child how they are in the world. Some of these identifications and internalizations can become schemas, when the learning that occurs fails to meet core emotional needs in the observing child. For example, a young girl raised by a hypervigilant, overly anxious mother may not experience any direct deficit, trauma, or over-indulgence, but is being taught that the world is dangerous or unmanageable. In an indirect manner, she is deprived of a secure base – not because of a weak parent–child bond, but because the parent herself feels insecure.

Other factors, beyond early environment, can play an important role in the development of schemas. These can include the child's emotional temperament, as well as the cultural context within which the child and the family live. Schemas ultimately emerge from the interaction of a child's temperament with his formative environment. Among the various temperamental vulnerabilities are biased/deficient information processing, emotion dysregulation, or disrupted interpersonal behavior. Schemas may emerge even in individuals without temperamental vulnerability, if faced with particularly toxic family environments or harsh life circumstances; however, the greater the temperamental vulnerability, the less environmental contribution needed.

Schemas create a sense of cognitive consistency – of a world that is predictable (if not controllable). And because people strive for this sort of predictability, schemas prove to be very durable; in a sense, schemas fight for their own survival. Our schemas are what we know – even if they torment us, they do so in ways that are somewhat familiar and comforting. They feel "right." Cognitively, schemas draw our attention to information that is consistent with the schema itself, and make us remember things in ways that "fit" with the schema. Behaviorally, they lead us to be drawn to certain familiar events. These cognitive and behavioral processes are responsible for schema maintenance – the self-perpetuating way in which long-established schemas keep a stronghold on our sensibility, influence how we think, feel, act, and relate to others, and paradoxically lead us to inadvertently recreate in our adult lives the conditions in childhood that were most harmful to us.

Schemas have their root in actual childhood or adolescent experience, and to a large degree, accurately reflect the tone of a person's early environment. For example, if a patient tells us that his family was cold and unaffectionate when he was young, he is usually correct, even though he may not understand why his parents had difficulty showing affection or expressing feelings. His attributions for their behavior may be wrong, but his basic sense of the emotional climate and how he was treated is almost always valid. Importantly, these early environments are ones over which the young child or adolescent has little influence – they are not the ones who create the particular emotional climate; instead, they are the ones whose needs are not met.

Later in life, schemas become dysfunctional because (a) cognitively and emotionally, they render all new situations, even ones that are profoundly different from the toxic early experiences, similarly toxic (even when in reality they are not), and (b) behaviorally and interpersonally, they lead the person to maintain particular types of environments or relationships, even when they can exert influence or choice and create other kinds of experiences.

Early maladaptive schemas, and the maladaptive ways patients learn to cope with them, often underlie chronic Axis I symptoms such as anxiety, depression, substance abuse, and psychosomatic disorders. They also underlie chronic Axis II symptoms such as dependence, avoidance, attention seeking, or perfectionism. Schemas are cognitive-affective traits, and as such, are dimensional: each exists on a continuum ranging in severity and pervasiveness. The more severe the schema, the more easily it becomes activated (triggered) and the more intense its consequences are. For example, if an individual experiences early and profound abandonment or invalidation that occurs in frequent and extreme ways and is carried out by both parents, their Abandonment and Emotional Deprivation schemas are likely to be triggered in many situations. As a consequence, they are likely to anticipate rejection at most times, to perceive it as present with very little evidence, and to respond strongly to it because of the intense and enduring distress it creates in them. In contrast, if an individual experienced relatively minor invalidation that occurred later in childhood, was milder, and was carried out only by one parent or by some (but not all) peers, their relevant schemas are likely to be less easily triggered and to lead to more moderate reactions. As a consequence, only strongly relevant events (e.g., criticism or disrespect from demanding authority figures of the invalidating parent's gender) may trigger the schemas.

# 3

## A taxonomy of early maladaptive schemas

Schemas emerge from unmet core emotional needs early in life. Because schemas maintain and perpetuate themselves, they continue to prevent the same needs from being met in adulthood. In this Point, we detail a list of 18 early maladaptive schemas that we have identified. We classify them according to five domains of unmet core needs to which they are most strongly related. The domains are hypothetical, and simply serve as a heuristic for organizing the various needs.

### *Domain I: DISCONNECTION AND REJECTION*

The first domain involves schemas related to violations of the basic universal needs for security, safety, stability, nurturance, empathy, sharing of feelings, acceptance, and respect. Schemas in this domain often emerge when early family environment is detached, withholding, cold, rejecting, violent, explosive, unpredictable, or abusive. Five schemas are tied to this domain:

#### *1. Abandonment/Instability*

This schema involves the perception that others, particularly those from whom we expect support and connection, are unstable and/or unreliable in providing these, and will not be able to continue providing emotional support, connection, strength, or practical protection. Family environments involving frequent angry outbursts, caregivers who were only erratically present, or parental figures who left or died an untimely death are common precursors to this schema.

### *2. Mistrust/Abuse*

This schema involves the expectation that others will hurt, abuse, humiliate, cheat, lie, manipulate, or take advantage of you. It usually involves the perception that the harm is intentional or the result of unjustified and extreme negligence. It may include the sense that one always ends up being cheated relative to others or "getting the short end of the stick."

### *3. Emotional Deprivation*

This schema involves the expectation that one's desire for a normal degree of emotional support will not be adequately met by others. There are three major forms of deprivation:

(a) Deprivation of Nurturance: Absence of attention, affection, warmth, or companionship
(b) Deprivation of Empathy: Absence of understanding, listening, self-disclosure, or mutual sharing of feelings from others
(c) Deprivation of Protection: Absence of strength, direction, or guidance from others.

### *4. Defectiveness/Shame*

This schema involves the feeling that one is fundamentally defective, bad, unwanted, inferior, or invalid in important respects, or that one would be unlovable to significant others if they could see the real self. It may involve hypersensitivity to criticism, rejection, and blame; self-consciousness, comparisons, and insecurity around others; or a sense of shame regarding one's perceived flaws. These flaws may be private (e.g., selfishness, angry impulses, unacceptable sexual desires) or public (e.g., undesirable physical appearance, social awkwardness).

### *5. Social Isolation/Alienation*

The feeling that one is isolated from the rest of the world, especially the social world outside the family. Individuals with this schema feel different from other people, and/or not part of any group or community. Though this schema reflects the same unmet needs (for safety, stability, and acceptance) as the other four in this domain, it typically comes about as a result of social exclusion outside the home environment (though at times, this social exclusion can be traced back to parental influences: a lack of encouragement for socializing, intense shame about one's home and background, or a sense of defectiveness and unlovability that emerges within the family of origin but is generalized to other situations).

## *Domain II: IMPAIRED AUTONOMY AND PERFORMANCE*

The second domain involves schemas related to violations of the basic universal needs for autonomy and competence, which lead to expectations about oneself and the environment that interfere with one's perceived ability to separate, survive, function independently, and perform successfully. Schemas in this domain often emerge when early family environment is enmeshed, undermining of the child's confidence, overprotective, or failing to reinforce the child for performing competently outside the family. Four schemas are tied to this domain:

### *6. Dependence/Incompetence*

This schema involves the belief that one is unable to handle one's everyday responsibilities in a competent manner, without considerable help from others. In extreme cases, individuals might feel unable to take care of themselves, solve daily problems, exercise good judgment, tackle new tasks, or make good decisions. In other cases, this sense of helplessness may be more circumscribed and be activated in particular situations or settings (e.g., in making important professional decisions or in choosing a partner).

### *7. Vulnerability to Harm or Illness*

This schema involves an exaggerated fear that catastrophe is imminent, that it will strike at any time, and that one will be unable to prevent it. The catastrophes that are anticipated are external in nature – and may focus on one or more of the following: (a) medical catastrophes: e.g., heart attacks, AIDS; (b) emotional catastrophes: e.g., going crazy; (c) external catastrophes: e.g., elevators collapsing, victimized by criminals, airplane crashes, earthquakes.

### *8. Enmeshment/Undeveloped Self*

This schema involves excessive emotional involvement and closeness with one or more significant others (often parents), at the expense of full individuation or normal social development. It often involves the belief that at least one of the enmeshed individuals cannot survive or be happy without the constant support of the other. It may also include feelings of being smothered by, or fused with, others or of insufficient individual identity. This schema is often experienced as feelings of emptiness and floundering, having no direction, or in extreme cases questioning one's existence.

### *9. Failure*

This schema involves the belief that one has failed, will inevitably fail, or is fundamentally inadequate relative to one's peers, in areas of achievement (school, career, sports, etc.). It often involves beliefs that one is stupid, inept, untalented, ignorant, lower in status, less successful than others, etc.

## *Domain III: IMPAIRED LIMITS*

The third domain involves schemas related to deficiencies in internal limits, responsibility towards others, or long-term goal-orientation. Schemas in this domain often lead to difficulties respecting the rights of others, cooperating with them, making commitments, or setting and meeting realistic personal goals. These schemas often emerge when early family environment is characterized by permissiveness, overindulgence, lack of direction, or a sense of superiority. Often, such families lacked appropriate confrontation, discipline, or limit-setting, and did not model behaviors such as taking responsibility, cooperating in a reciprocal manner, or setting goals. In some cases, the child may not have been expected to tolerate normal levels of discomfort, or may not have been given adequate supervision, direction, or guidance. Two schemas are tied to this domain:

### *10. Entitlement/Grandiosity*

This schema involves the belief that one is superior to other people, entitled to special rights and privileges, or not bound by the rules of reciprocity that guide normal social interaction. The schema often involves insistence that one should be able to do or have whatever one wants, regardless of what is realistic, what others consider reasonable, or what costs others may bear. In some cases, the schema involves an exaggerated focus on superiority (e.g., being among the most successful, famous, wealthy) – in order to achieve power or control (not primarily for attention or approval). At times, it includes excessive competitiveness toward, or domination of, others, in one of several ways – asserting one's power, forcing one's point of view, or controlling the behavior of others in line with one's own desires – without empathy or concern for others' needs or feelings.

### *11. Insufficient Self-control/Self-discipline*

This schema involves a pervasive difficulty or refusal to exercise sufficient self-control and frustration tolerance to achieve one's personal goals, or to restrain the excessive expression of one's emotions and impulses. In its milder form, patients present with an exaggerated emphasis on avoiding discomfort: avoiding pain, conflict, confrontation, responsibility, or overexertion – at the expense of personal fulfillment, commitment, or integrity.

## *Domain IV: OTHER-DIRECTEDNESS*

The fourth domain involves schemas related to deficits in the fulfillment of the basic universal need for self-directness. Such deficits lead to an excessive focus on the desires, feelings, and responses of others, at the expense of one's own needs. This focus is driven by the need to gain love and approval, maintain a sense of connection or belonging, or avoid retaliation. These schemas usually involve a suppression or lack of awareness regarding one's own emotions, needs, or wishes, and lead to difficulties in assertion or self-determination. They often emerge when children are brought up in an atmosphere of conditional positive regard or conditional acceptance: the child needed to suppress important aspects of the self in order to gain love, attention, or approval. In many cases, the parents' emotional needs and desires – or social acceptance and status – were valued more than the unique needs and feelings of each child. Three schemas are tied to this domain:

### *12. Subjugation*

This schema involves an excessive degree of relinquishing control to others because one feels coerced to do so to avoid anger, retaliation, or abandonment. The two major forms of subjugation are:

(a) Subjugation of Needs: Suppression of one's preferences, decisions, and desires.
(b) Subjugation of Emotions: Suppression of emotional expression, especially anger.

The Subjugation schema usually involves the perception that one's own desires, opinions, and feelings are not valid or important to others. The schema frequently presents as excessive compliance, combined with hypersensitivity to feeling trapped. It generally leads to a build-up of anger, manifested in maladaptive symptoms (e.g., passive–aggressive behavior, uncontrolled outbursts of temper, psychosomatic symptoms, withdrawal of affection, "acting out," or substance abuse).

### *13. Self-sacrifice*

This schema involves an excessive focus on voluntarily meeting the needs of others, at the expense of one's own gratification. Some common motivations for behavior that is consistent with this schema are avoiding actions that may cause pain to others, avoiding guilt from feeling selfish, or maintaining a connection with others who are perceived as needy. This schema often results from an acute sensitivity to the pain of others, and at times, leads to a sense that one's own needs are not being adequately met and to resentment of those receiving one's care.

### *14. Approval-seeking/Recognition-seeking*

This schema involves an excessive emphasis on gaining approval, recognition, or attention from other people, or on fitting in, at the expense of developing a secure and true sense of self. For individuals with this schema, one's sense of esteem is dependent primarily on the reactions of others rather than on one's own natural inclinations. The schema sometimes includes an overemphasis on status, appearance, social acceptance, money, or achievement – as means of gaining approval, admiration, or attention (but not primarily for power or control). It often results in major life decisions that are inauthentic or unsatisfying, or in hypersensitivity to rejection.

### *Domain V: OVERVIGILANCE AND INHIBITION*

The fifth domain involves schemas related to violations of the basic universal need for spontaneity and playfulness. These violations may result in an excessive emphasis on suppressing one's spontaneous feelings, impulses, or choices. They also may result in a perpetual focus on meeting rigid, internalized rules and expectations about performance and ethical behavior, often at the expense of happiness, self-expression, relaxation, close relationships, or health. These schemas often emerge from a family atmosphere that is grim, demanding, and sometimes punitive. In such families, performance, obligations, duties, and rule-bound behavior often predominate over pleasure, relaxation, or playfulness. Children are often expected to hide emotions, avoid mistakes, and strive for perfection. There is usually an undercurrent of pessimism and worry – that things could fall apart if one fails to be vigilant and careful at all times. Four schemas are tied to this domain:

#### *15. Negativity/Pessimism*

This schema involves a pervasive, lifelong focus on the negative aspects of life (pain, death, loss, disappointment, conflict, guilt, resentment, unsolved problems, potential mistakes, betrayal, things that could go wrong, etc.) while minimizing or neglecting the positive or optimistic aspects. It usually includes an exaggerated expectation that things will eventually go seriously wrong in a wide range of work, financial, or interpersonal situations, or that aspects of one's life that seem to be going well will ultimately fall apart. Usually, it involves an inordinate fear of making mistakes that might lead to financial collapse, loss, humiliation, or to being trapped in a bad situation.

Because potential negative outcomes are exaggerated, individuals with this schema are frequently characterized by chronic worry, vigilance, complaining, or indecision.

### *16. Emotional Inhibition*

This schema involves the excessive inhibition of spontaneous action, feeling, or communication – usually to avoid disapproval by others, feelings of shame, or losing control of one's impulses. The most common areas of inhibition involve: (a) inhibition of anger and aggression; (b) inhibition of positive impulses (e.g., joy, affection, sexual excitement, play); (c) difficulty expressing vulnerability or communicating freely about one's feelings, needs, etc.; or (d) excessive emphasis on rationality while disregarding emotions.

### *17. Unrelenting Standards/Hypercriticalness*

This schema involves the underlying belief that one must strive to meet very high internalized standards of behavior and performance, usually to avoid criticism. It typically results in feelings of pressure or difficulty slowing down, and in hypercriticalness toward oneself and others. It invariably involves significant impairment in pleasure, relaxation, health, self-esteem, sense of accomplishment, or satisfying relationships.

Unrelenting standards typically present as: (a) perfectionism, inordinate attention to detail, or an underestimate of how good one's own performance is relative to the norm; (b) rigid rules and "shoulds" in many areas of life, including unrealistically high moral, ethical, cultural, or religious precepts; or (c) preoccupation with time and efficiency, so that more can be accomplished.

### *18. Punitiveness*

This schema involves the belief that people (including oneself) should be harshly punished for making mistakes. It involves the tendency to be angry, intolerant, punitive, and impatient with any person who does not meet one's expectations or standards. The schema usually includes difficulty forgiving mistakes committed by oneself or others because of a reluctance to consider extenuating circumstances, allow for human imperfection, or empathize with feelings.

4

## Coping styles and responses

Why are schemas so difficult to change? What explains their tenaciousness? For one thing, schemas tend to be self-perpetuating. People tend to rely on their existing schemas to make sense of new information, a process that Jean Piaget (1955) called *assimilation*. Only when information is so discrepant that it can no longer be assimilated into existing schemas are people forced to modify their schemas, a complementary process known as *accommodation* (Piaget, 1955). Thus, schemas are inherently conservative. People tend to hold onto their existing views of themselves, other people, and the world, despite contradictory evidence. Moreover, schemas filter the information we receive (Beck, Freeman, & Davis, 2003; Young et al., 2003). We focus on information that is consistent with our schemas, and tend to ignore or disregard that which is inconsistent. For example, Sara, a woman with a strong Defectiveness schema, felt sure that her friends didn't really like her, despite the abundant evidence that they valued her for her warmth, caring, loyalty, and generosity. Instead, she focused on her shortcomings, and discounted the positive feedback she received from others (e.g., "If they really knew me well, they'd think otherwise").

People also tend to behave, consciously or unconsciously, in ways which perpetuate their schemas. For example, our emotional and sexual "chemistry" with other people is often based on the schemas that they activate in us, and vice versa (see Point 27). We may be attracted to "bad boys" or "bad girls" because they seem dangerous, alluring, distant, powerful, or exciting. This high level of chemistry can be a reflection of our schemas. The "strong, silent type" may be attractive because we want to break through his or her emotional reserve. However, at core, this attraction may reflect an Emotional Deprivation schema, an expectation that others will inevitably neglect our needs for love, affection, and attention. Thus, we choose "high chemistry" partners who unconsciously activate and perpetuate these same schemas: a distant partner who reinforces an Emotional Deprivation schema; an unreliable partner who reinforces an Abandonment schema; or an abusive partner who reinforces a Mistrust/Abuse schema.

Finally, people tend to cope with their schemas in ways that reinforce them. When schemas are activated, they provoke strong emotions such as fear, anger, sadness, shame, or guilt. People cope with this schematic activation in three broad ways or "coping styles": *schema surrender*, *schema avoidance*, and *schema overcompensation*. Schema surrender means giving in to one's schemas; schema avoidance means avoiding people or situations that trigger one's schemas; schema overcompensation means doing the opposite of one's schemas. Young et al. (2003) distinguish between coping styles and coping responses. Coping styles are broad tendencies to cope with schematic activation, using surrender, avoidance, or overcompensation. Coping responses are the individual ways in which these broad tendencies can manifest themselves. For example, an avoidant coping style might manifest itself in a range of avoidant strategies or behaviors: avoiding thinking about upsetting things, avoiding people or situations that might trigger one's schemas, using drugs or alcohol as ways of blocking feelings, and so forth. Thus, the avoidant coping style, which represents a broad tendency to avoid, can manifest itself in a variety of specific avoidant coping responses.

Coping styles and responses typically originate in childhood as attempts to adapt to challenging life circumstances. However, despite their original adaptive value, they eventually become inflexible and maladaptive. For example, as a young girl, Judith learned to stay in her room and immerse herself in books when her parents were fighting. Her withdrawal into reading was an adaptive response to a frightening and painful situation in which she, like most children, had limited control over her environment. However, over time, this tendency crystallized into an avoidant style, a generalized tendency to avoid stressful or emotional situations that left her unable to deal effectively with many life circumstances, and served to reinforce her schemas. Her unmet needs for closeness and belonging (which developed into Emotional Deprivation and Social Isolation schemas, respectively) were reinforced by her tendency to avoid any situation in which connection and intimacy might be possible. She refused to let others get to know her, which eventually discouraged potential friends and romantic partners from getting close to her. Thus, her avoidant coping style, while rooted in understandable attempts to escape from the painful circumstances of her childhood, only reinforced the very schemas that made it so difficult for her to get her emotional needs met.

Some patients with personality disorders have a predominant style of coping. For example, patients with narcissistic personality disorder use a predominantly overcompensating style, while those with avoidant personality disorder have an avoidant style. However, most patients utilize more than one coping style. For example, though a man with narcissistic personality disorder may have a dominant, arrogant style (i.e., an overcompensating coping style) towards people that he perceives to be lower on the social hierarchy, he may behave in a submissive manner towards those whom he perceives to be superior to him (i.e., a surrender coping style) in an effort to gain approval or avoid disapproval.

Furthermore, coping responses may change over the lifespan. For instance, in their youth, some patients with borderline personality disorder choose unreliable, untrustworthy partners who end up mistreating or abandoning them. Thus, they unconsciously surrender to their schemas of Abandonment, Mistrust/Abuse, Defectiveness, and Emotional Deprivation, and intensify these schemas. After many painful, failed relationships, these patients may foreswear relationships altogether, because they are sure that they will inevitably be hurt or abandoned again. Thus, the predominant coping style shifts from surrender to avoidance, though the underlying schemas remain the same.

The incorporation of coping styles into the Schema Therapy model of personality disorders represents a departure from traditional cognitive theories, such as those of Beck et al. (2003). While traditional cognitive models focus on "core beliefs," which bear some similarity to the concept of early maladaptive schemas, Young et al. (2003) argue that the behavioral adaptation of individuals with the same schemas may differ markedly from one another, depending on the coping styles that they use. For example, three people with a Defectiveness schema might adapt to this schema in fundamentally different ways. One develops an arrogant, superior manner that hides his underlying feelings of inferiority (overcompensating coping style). The second unconsciously sabotages himself, setting himself up for failure or embarrassment that reinforces his sense of inferiority (surrender coping style). The third may cope with his inferiority feelings by avoiding people or situations that trigger them, such as those he perceives to be more successful or attractive than he is (avoidant coping style). Thus, in the Schema Therapy model, the combination of dysfunctional schemas and maladaptive coping responses forms the conceptual core of personality disorders.

The concept of coping styles bears similarity to the psychodynamic notion of defense mechanisms, particularly as formulated by the so-called "ego psychologists" or "neo-Freudians," who emphasized the adaptive side of defenses. For example, Karen Horney (1946) described three "coping strategies": "moving towards people," "moving against people," and "moving away from people." These coping strategies correspond roughly to the coping styles of surrender, overcompensation, and avoidance described in Schema Therapy. However, Young et al.'s (2003) formulation differs from that of Horney and other ego-psychologists in important ways. Young et al.'s model is not based on the idea of unconscious mental conflicts between drives (e.g., sex and aggression) and defenses, which is central to psychodynamic conceptions of defense mechanisms. Moreover, it does not include the idea of mental contents, such as unacceptable sexual or aggressive wishes, that are kept unconscious through the force of repression. Instead, we speak of schemas and coping responses being triggered unconsciously, only in the sense that they represent largely automatic reactions that occur without conscious awareness. This is consistent with recent cognitive theory and research, which indicates that much of mental processing occurs at an unconscious, implicit level (Uhlmann, Pizarro, & Bloom, 2008). However, in Young et al.'s model, as in the rest of cognitive psychology, there is no concept of unconscious drives or wishes being kept from consciousness by a repressive barrier.

Young et al. (2003) suggest that the coping styles of overcompensation, avoidance, and surrender may be rooted in our evolutionary heritage, as indicated by the capacity of humans and other living organisms to "fight," "flee," or "freeze," in response to danger. Evolutionary psychologists, such as Hans Eysenck and Jeffrey Gray, have theorized that individual differences in personality traits such as introversion/extraversion (Eysenck, 1990) and behavioral activation/inhibition (Gray, 1990) may be rooted in our biological make-up. Thus, coping styles such as overcompensation and avoidance may be related to inherited biological dispositions to approach or avoid, respectively. In the Schema Therapy model, however, these individual differences in coping style are not only a reflection of innate behavioral mechanisms. Life experiences can also shape these tendencies, for example, through modeling or reinforcement. For example, an emotionally neglected child may learn to attract the attention of others by being charming, entertaining, or seductive, thus forming the basis of an overcompensating coping style. The attention the child receives reinforces her own innate tendency towards extraversion. Thus, the coping style that the child eventually develops represents an interaction between inherited, biological disposition, and life experiences.

# 5

## Coping styles: Surrender responses

The surrender coping style is the tendency to give in to one's schemas. Unlike the overcompensating and avoidant coping styles, in which painful feelings are escaped from or avoided altogether, a person with this style feels the pain of the schemas directly. However, instead of fighting against the schemas in a healthy way, the surrendering person submits to them, passively and helplessly giving into them.

The surrender coping style is perhaps the most difficult of the coping styles to comprehend. Why would people give in to their schemas when doing so leads to increased emotional pain? It seems counterintuitive that people would be drawn to those who mistreat them, stay in relationships in which their needs are chronically unmet, or persist in activities that are chronically unsatisfying. Yet, we frequently see examples of schema surrender in clinical practice, as well as in daily life. Psychoanalysts refer to these phenomena as the "repetition-compulsion," and link them to past trauma. The compulsion to repeat past painful events in present memory or behavior is seen as an attempt at mastering them (Loewald, 1980). Elsewhere, psychoanalysts also described some self-defeating behavior as a form of masochism – an unconscious pleasure in pain (Freud, 1924).

In contrast, Schema Therapy posits no unconscious masochistic needs. From a Schema Therapy point of view, people who surrender are simply stuck in patterns that prevent them from getting their emotional needs met. Their schemas distort the way in which they see painful situations, making it difficult to find more healthy alternatives. Moreover, when people surrender to their schemas, they cope with their schemas by playing passive, compliant, or dependent roles, in which they feel and act almost child-like in relationships with other adults whom they perceive to be stronger or more self-assured than they are. These behaviors may temporarily make them feel safer, but ultimately leave them feeling even more miserable.

For example, Pauline felt intense feelings of shame and inferiority in social situations (Defectiveness/Shame schema). She dreaded being in social groups, where she felt awkward and stupid. She felt that she lacked the social graces that others took for granted. She always managed to say or do the wrong thing, embarrassing herself, then blushing and lapsing into silence. She spent hours scrutinizing her behavior after such encounters, wincing as she recalled every shameful moment. She coped by surrendering to her schemas. Rather than fighting her Defectiveness schema, she gave into it, feeling more and more inferior and humiliated with each social encounter.

Pauline's boyfriend dominated their relationship. Outwardly self-assured, even arrogant, he also had a Defectiveness schema for which he overcompensated by choosing partners who were more insecure than himself. At times, the boyfriend played the role of the protective parent, reassuring Pauline when she felt bad and giving her advice. She grew to depend on him to help her make even small decisions, like where to go to dinner or which movies to see, because she felt incompetent to make such decisions herself (surrendering to a Dependence/Incompetence schema). At other times, the boyfriend lost his patience with Pauline's incessant need for reassurance; he would scold her and leave her in tears, suffering from the familiar feeling of being an unwanted burden to him. In these ways and others, Pauline's surrender coping style reinforced her schemas of Defectiveness and Incompetence.

The surrender coping style is often seen in connection with schemas in the "Other-directedness" domain: Approval-seeking, Self-sacrifice, and Subjugation. People with these schemas are overly focused on the needs of other people to the exclusion of their own needs. They often cope with these schemas by surrendering to them: working too hard to earn others' approval, giving too much to others while sacrificing their own needs, and subjugating themselves to others' demands.

# 6

## Coping styles: Avoidant responses

Avoidant coping responses involve an avoidance of people or situations that trigger one's schemas. In some people, an avoidant style of coping can be quite pervasive, significantly interfering with their ability to get the love they need, achieve satisfaction at work, or derive pleasure from everyday activities. Clara, a woman in her late forties, had studied law as a young woman. She had a severe Unrelenting Standards schema, and felt that earning anything less than "straight A's" in her courses would make her a failure. She worked extremely long hours compared with her law school colleagues, shunning any sort of social contact or pleasurable activities so that she could concentrate exclusively on her work. She did achieve her goal of earning straight A's, but at a high price: after two years of this demanding regime, she "burned out," and had to drop out of law school. The shame she felt after this perceived "failure" was intense. When she was able to return to work, she chose a job that was undemanding but extremely tedious: working as a legal assistant editing technical documents. She hated her job, but stayed at it for 10 years. She often talked about leaving to find other employment but was terrified of taking a risk that would lead to another failure like the one she had experienced in law school. She had long ago foresworn romantic relationships because of the pain they caused. She had few friends and lived alone with her sister who was disabled and needed constant care and attention.

Thus, Clara had an avoidant coping style that manifested itself in pervasive and extreme restrictions in nearly every area of her life. Although these restrictions made her quite miserable, in her mind, they were preferable to the pain that she believed would inevitably occur if she were to take more risks. She avoided any situation that might activate her schemas of Defectiveness, Failure, and Unrelenting Standards.

Avoidant coping responses are quite common, even if not always as pervasive or severe as in the above example. They are often, though by no means exclusively, seen in anxiety disorders, such as simple phobia, social phobia, agoraphobia, or post-traumatic stress disorder, or in the so-called "Cluster C" personality disorders (i.e., avoidant, dependent, and obsessive-compulsive personality disorders) on Axis II of the DSM-IV (APA, 2000). However, avoidant coping responses can be associated with nearly any disorder on Axis I or Axis II.

An often-overlooked feature of avoidant responses is how difficult they can be to change. A principal reason for this is that avoidant coping responses are self-reinforcing via a form of operant conditioning known as *negative reinforcement* (Skinner, 1953). In negative reinforcement, behavior is strengthened when a feared situation is escaped from or avoided. Avoidant coping responses temporarily lessen the unpleasant feelings that are associated with schematic activation, producing a sensation of relief. However, this temporary respite from fear or pain is self-perpetuating, in that it "rewards" the same avoidant behavior that produced it. In other words, avoidant coping responses lessen anxiety in the short run, but strengthen avoidant behavior and anxiety in the long run.

People with an avoidant coping style may engage in cognitive as well as behavioral avoidance (Borkovec, Alcaine, & Behar, 2004): i.e., they may avoid thinking about or remembering situations that might trigger their schemas. For example, Ira lived far away from his family and would rarely see them, even for holidays. He said that, when growing up, his family had been a depressing one where "no one had any fun." In fact, he had a strong Emotional Deprivation schema, having had a rejecting father and a mother who, though caring, was too focused on the details of running the household to pay attention to the emotional needs of her children. Ira claimed not to think about his parents or siblings very much, asking what the point was of dwelling on the past. He preferred to fill up his time with fun activities like riding his mountain bike and living a lavish lifestyle of fine wine, gourmet meals, and fancy parties. When he met a woman who was stable and nurturing, he began to fall in love. However, when she mentioned her desire to have children, he quickly broke off the relationship. At the age of 50, he was still a fun-loving bachelor who felt that it was pointless to dwell on the negative. Thus, in addition to avoiding situations that triggered his schemas, such as visiting family or forming a committed relationship, he engaged in pervasive cognitive avoidance. He quickly pushed away any thought or recollection that might trigger painful feelings by distracting himself with his many pleasant pastimes. Thus, Ira's avoidance, while temporarily distracting him from his inner pain, left him with a sense of inner loneliness and emptiness.

7

# Coping styles: Overcompensation responses

Overcompensating coping responses represent attempts to "do the opposite" of schemas. A child who is neglected (and who has developed an Emotional Deprivation schema) may learn to capture the attention of others by being charming, flirty, or theatrical. A child who feels deep shame or worthlessness (Defectiveness/Shame schema) may be driven to succeed by outworking others, or may develop a dominant, aggressive style that helps him reach the top. A child who is bullied or abused may become a bully herself, hiding her fear (Vulnerability to Harm schema) behind a façade of toughness.

Overcompensating coping responses are a prominent feature of many patients with the "Cluster B" or dramatic cluster personality disorders. The narcissistic personality disorder is perhaps the prototype of the overcompensating coping style. Individuals with narcissistic personality disorder are preoccupied with status, beauty, or success, view themselves as special or superior, and look down on others whom they see as "ordinary" (Ronningstam, 2009). Many theorists have speculated that narcissistic individuals develop a grandiose self-image as a means of overcompensating for underlying feelings of emptiness, loneliness, or inferiority (Ronningstam, 2009; Young & Flanagan, 1998). These individuals often report being raised by parents who ignored their basic emotional needs, while using the child to satisfy their own egoistic needs. Thus, the child comes to place an inordinate emphasis on outward status, glamour, or achievement, but at the same time feels an inner sense of emptiness or inferiority.

The overcompensating style can be seen quite clearly in the case of Harry, a successful real-estate agent who moved in rich and glamorous circles. Harry's life was a series of social events. When a new girlfriend entered his life, she would often find this aspect exciting at first, but would eventually notice that Harry put severe restrictions on their own relationship. He would only see her on weekends because of his busy schedule. He became irritated when called during the week and eventually forbade her from doing so.

It took a long time for Harry's vulnerable side to become apparent. He was excessively concerned with his appearance. Every hair had to be neatly in place before he would appear in public. In fact, he was actually quite anxious about failing or being rejected. Periodically, when things weren't going well for him, he could get quite depressed. Although there were moments when Harry shared his feelings with his girlfriend, these were few and far between. Normally, he maintained a chilly distance, while relentlessly criticizing her for her supposed shortcomings. Eventually, she grew tired of her boyfriend's arrogance, emotional aloofness, and excessive control, and broke off the relationship.

This case illustrates the narcissist's use of overcompensation – a superior, arrogant, and devaluing stance towards others – that tries, but ultimately fails, to make up for feelings of loneliness or inferiority.

Overcompensating responses may temporarily alleviate some of the emotional pain connected to schemas; however, they do not "cure" schemas. The overcompensator may feel "on top of the world" after experiencing a new triumph, but the underlying schemas remain. Patients with overcompensating styles frequently believe that the opposite is true. For example, Jason, a narcissistic attorney, told his therapist that all of his problems would be solved if he could only make enough money, and spend the rest of his life playing golf. However, when narcissistic individuals experience a serious failure or disappointment, their schemas can become triggered, and the overcompensating nature of their grandiosity is exposed.

Over-control is another form of overcompensating response. As in narcissistic overcompensation, the excessive need for control develops as a way of overcompensating for schemas. For example, Edgar, a prominent physician, had lost both of his parents to illness as a child. He had to "grow up quickly," learning to take responsibility at a young age. As an adult, he was often described by others as a "control freak." He was obsessed with neatness and order. He would become unnerved if someone moved a pile of papers on his desk or disrupted his carefully scheduled routine. He was highly driven, tightly wound, and lacked spontaneity. He became the chief of surgery at a hospital. His penchant for order, attention to detail, and perfectionism helped him to succeed in this demanding job. At the same time, his controlling, demanding nature drove his colleagues crazy. Eventually, his marriage fell apart because of his workaholism. Thus, his overcompensating style had both adaptive and maladaptive aspects. It helped him to succeed at work, but at a very high price. His over-control was rooted in Abandonment and Vulnerability to Harm schemas: an expectation that devastating illnesses or other catastrophes could strike at any moment, leaving him helpless and alone, as indeed they had when he had lost both of his parents at an age when he was ill prepared to cope with it. His over-control was an attempt to prevent such catastrophes from occurring by maintaining complete control over his environment.

Aggression can also serve as a form of overcompensation. Children who are abused or bullied may "turn the tables" by taking the role of abuser or bully. Ryan, a man who was incarcerated for assault, described this process. He had been viciously beaten by his father throughout his childhood and adolescence. Finally, after enduring many beatings, he suddenly fought back, catching his father by surprise, and savagely beat him. He joined a gang of delinquent youths who roved the streets, looking for victims to beat and rob. He felt powerful and invulnerable. During Schema Therapy, his pervasive mistrust of others (Mistrust/Abuse schema) was evident. Eventually, he began, for the first time in years, to feel anxiety, an emotion that he connected to the terror he had experienced with his father. Thus, his aggression served an overcompensating function: it protected him from the terrifying vulnerability he had experienced as a child.

8

## Schema modes as states (the state vs. trait distinction)

A major development in the evolution of Schema Therapy was the introduction of the *mode* concept. Modes refer to the predominant emotional state, schemas, and coping reactions that are active for an individual at a particular time. By definition, modes are transient states. This is in contrast to schemas which can be thought of as traits – stable characteristics of the person. At any given moment, a person is predominantly in one particular mode. In social-cognitive terms, we could think of that mode as the working self-concept – the part of the person's self or identity which is primed or active at the moment – and which drives the way they anticipate, see, and respond to the world around them. There are four main types of modes:

(a) Child modes
(b) Maladaptive coping modes
(c) Dysfunctional internalized parent modes, and
(d) A healthy adult mode.

We devote the next several points to an elaborate description of these modes. Particular attention is given to what we see as the wounded core of the individual and a key target in therapy, namely the Vulnerable Child mode (Point 9). Point 10 addresses other child modes that are often the target of therapy (namely, Angry and Impulsive Child modes). Points 11 and 12, respectively, discuss maladaptive coping modes and internalized parent modes. Finally, Point 13 groups together two healthy modes: the healthy adult and the contented child.

Every person has the capacity to be in a variety of modes over the course of their day or week, and certainly throughout their lifetime. What differentiates us are both the specific modes that are particularly common, and the manner in which we transition from one mode to another.

At the extreme, modes could be almost entirely dissociated from one another, leading to the clinical presentation of dissociative identity disorder. Several personality disorders are thought to lie at a less extreme, but still pathological, level of dissociation among modes. Indeed, the mode concept was first introduced following the realization that for certain patients – especially ones with the characteristic features of borderline personality or narcissistic personality – trait-like schemas (which are stable and pervasive) leave unexplained many of the more fast-changing symptoms (which are unstable and temporary). Patients with these personality features experience quick and often intense fluctuation among various mood states – in a sense, flipping among modes in response to external or internal triggers. Modes were introduced as a way of naming these states, and ultimately working with them clinically.

The more the patient is characterized by fluctuations among various states, the more room there is for mode work. But the mode concept and the techniques that make use of this concept are helpful not only in the treatment of patients with personality disorders; instead, they have become an integral part of Schema Therapy and are now fluidly blended into regular schema work (see Points 19 and 24).

Indeed, healthy persons also move between modes, but retain a unified sense of self, and can simultaneously experience blends of modes – that is, more than one mode at a time. When they do shift between modes, they do so gradually and not abruptly. They also have less difficulty recognizing and acknowledging their modes. For example, a healthy person would be able to say "I've been feeling more upset and needy" when they recognize being in a Vulnerable Child mode, and may be able to identify the triggers for the ascendance of this mode at that very moment.

In other words, Schema Therapy does not see pathology as qualitatively different from healthy functioning in this regard: all people have different sides of themselves; every person includes a multi-vocality of modes. What's lost in severe pathology is the ability to balance these modes, to reconcile their competing styles and impulses, and to transition seamlessly among them.

9

# The wounded core: Vulnerable Child mode

The first and possibly most important mode to consider clinically is the Vulnerable Child mode. This is the mode that usually experiences most of the core schemas. When we are in a Vulnerable Child mode, we are like lost or wounded children. We may appear sad and hopeless, or be anxious, overwhelmed, and helpless. As the name implies, we often feel weak, vulnerable, exposed, and defenseless. The Vulnerable Child is a remnant of the time when the person was a child needing the care of adults in order to survive, but was not getting that care.

The specific nature of the wound to the Vulnerable Child depends upon the needs that went unmet, and thus, on the predominant schema or schemas. Based on the specific nature, a more specific name (other than "Vulnerable Child") might be used for the mode. For example, if a child was often left alone or had parental figures whose presence was unpredictable, the Abandonment schema may predominate and we would refer to the vulnerability as the "Abandoned Child." Loneliness, sadness, and isolation may be the key feelings in this case. If the child was subjected to direct cruelty or violence, the Mistrust/Abuse schema may predominate and the vulnerability will take the form we call "Abused Child." In this case, feelings of fear, fragility, and victimization may be the key feelings.

Other forms of the Vulnerable Child mode (e.g., the Deprived Child, the Defective Child, the Lost Child) reflect other predominant schemas (e.g., Emotional Deprivation, Defectiveness, and Enmeshment schemas, respectively). Indeed, most schemas are part of the Vulnerable Child mode. (The possible exceptions are those schemas tied to more acting-out behaviors, namely Entitlement and Insufficient Self-control. These schemas are tied more strongly to the Impulsive Child mode; see Point 10.) Because the Vulnerable Child mode "holds" most schemas, we regard it as the core mode for the purpose of schema work.

The ultimate objective of Schema Therapy is to help adults get their own needs met, even though these needs may have not been met in the past. The Vulnerable Child mode provides the clearest and most unequivocal manifestation of unmet needs and of their emotional consequences. Thus, it is this mode that we are most concerned with accessing and helping. In a nutshell, we are trying to heal the Vulnerable Child mode – and to teach the patient to gradually provide such self-nurturance on their own.

Importantly, the nurturance of the Vulnerable Child mode, and the access to the mode that it requires, are often quite difficult to achieve. The experiences of vulnerability and distress that are inherent to this mode are painful and patients often expend great effort to avoid or combat the mode. Most commonly, the patient would engage in some coping behaviors to escape the mode (see Point 11: Maladaptive coping modes). Alternatively, the patient may automatically revert to an internalized parent mode, reacting to, and exacerbating, the vulnerability (see Point 12: Internalized parent modes).

Ironically, these maladaptive coping efforts and reactions only increase and prolong the distress. The schema therapist's role is to gently encourage the patient to accept, and participate in, a counterintuitive process of recognizing and experiencing the vulnerability rather than pushing it away. If the vulnerability is kept hidden or obscured, no such process can take place: the schemas cannot heal unless the patient is in the Vulnerable Child mode. If it is allowed to come to the surface, the slow process of addressing it can occur.

We detail the clinical techniques that focus on accessing the vulnerable child in Points 23–27, particularly in Point 24, on the use of imagery to access the Vulnerable Child mode. In essence, all of these techniques work through the following three processes:

(1) Distinguishing "sad" from "bad" and separating self-criticism or self-blame (secondary emotions) from the more primary emotions
(2) Recognizing and expressing unmet needs as a precursor to having them met, and
(3) Beginning the processes of having the needs met within the therapy itself (i.e., the therapist's reparenting).

Compared with most other modes (namely, child modes such as the Angry or Impulsive Child; maladaptive coping modes such as the Detached Protector or the Compliant Surrenderer; and maladaptive internalized parent modes such as the Punitive Parent), the Vulnerable Child is a healthy mode to be in. The term "healthy" may seem confusing in this regard because of the intense distress that is experienced in this mode. However, Schema Therapy views the experience of (often painful) vulnerability as essential for the sake of ultimately healing the schemas and gaining the capacity for getting one's needs met.

A final point regarding the Vulnerable Child mode has to do with the age of that child. It is often useful to help patients identify how old they are (or how old they feel) when in this mode. For patients who are stronger and for whom therapy may use more schema (and not mode) techniques, the Vulnerable Child may be an older child or even an early adolescent. In contrast, for patients with borderline personality disorder, the Vulnerable Child is typically of a much younger age – often as young as 2–4 years. The age of the Vulnerable Child is reflected in its cognitive capacity, in its ability to verbalize feelings, and most importantly, in the types of needs that it has (and which were frustrated). For example, very young children lack object permanence and would have no capacity to engage in self-soothing or self-regulating behaviors when a caregiver is absent. They have little ability to summon up memories or to project into the future. Instead, they are often tempest-tossed by the present events in their lives or in the therapy sessions, feeling and reacting with intense emotions and with impulsive action to whatever is happening right then.

# 10

# Angry and Impulsive Child modes

## Angry Child mode

The Angry Child mode is the side of the person that feels and expresses anger or rage in response to unmet core needs. The Angry Child mode is evident in uncontrolled, or poorly controlled, expressions of anger. More extreme manifestations include screaming, shouting, swearing, throwing things, banging on things, or breaking things. Less extreme manifestations include having an angry or agitated facial expression or body language, or speaking in a loud or angry voice. Such reactions often seem disproportionate to the events that have triggered them, and usually involve some degree of schema-related distortion. Often, this state involves venting feelings about perceived unfairness or injustice. For example, a patient may become enraged at his therapist for arriving late for a session; a husband may rage at his wife for humiliating him; or a worker may lose control and lash out at his boss for not appreciating him. In many cases, such perceptions of injustice may involve a kernel of truth, that is, they are based in part on real injustices or unfairness. However, schema-related distortions explain much of the intensity of these reactions.

The Angry Child mode may be triggered by feelings of mistreatment (Mistrust/Abuse schema), abandonment (Abandonment schema), neglect (Emotional Deprivation schema), or humiliation (Defectiveness/Shame schema) in patients whose early emotional needs were chronically frustrated or went unmet. The Angry Child mode may also be triggered by feelings of frustration or impatience in patients whose sense of entitlement (Entitlement schema) or lack of self-control (Insufficient Self-control/Self-discipline schema) stems from spoiling or inadequate limit setting in childhood. Such individuals may flip into Angry Child mode when denied immediate gratification of their needs or desires.

When the Angry Child mode is triggered, it can look as if the person is having a temper tantrum: balled-up fists, red face, foot stomping, and so forth. As a result, such reactions are often counterproductive. They are perceived by others as childish and inappropriate, or as threatening and frightening, and can have negative consequences for relationships and in the workplace. In contrast, the healthy expression of anger involves the constructive expression of angry feelings within appropriate limits. It is a common misconception that anger per se is destructive. In fact, the healthy expression of anger can help to bring problems or conflicts to light, making it possible to resolve them. However, the person with a prominent Angry Child mode often lacks a strong Healthy Adult side that can modulate these reactions and channel them in constructive ways.

In extreme cases, individuals in an Angry Child mode may present a real danger to others (e.g., in cases of "road rage," domestic violence, or the physical abuse of children). In such instances, individuals may "see red," entering a dissociated state of rage in which they lose control and act out violently. Such individuals may describe their anger as explosive, going from "0 to 100" in the blink of an eye, with no middle ground in between.

Even when patients with an Angry Child mode are able to contain such reactions in the moment, they may continue to harbor resentments and ruminate over perceived wrongs, suggesting that the schemas involved in these reactions remain active. For example, Tom, an inpatient at a forensic hospital who had physically abused his girlfriend, described the constant feeling of having a "clenched fist" in the pit of his stomach. These pent-up feelings may lead to outbursts later, when they are triggered by an incident that often involves a schema-related theme.

### *Impulsive Child mode*

The Impulsive Child mode is a side of the patient that behaves impulsively, and has difficulty tolerating frustration. The Impulsive Child "wants what he wants when he wants it." They experience their needs as urgent and find it intolerable to wait to have their needs met or to have them denied. When the Impulsive Child wants something, he immediately springs into action without stopping to think about the possible consequences. Patients with an Impulsive Child mode lack a Healthy Adult side that can reflect on the pros and cons of behaviors, while simultaneously inhibiting impulses.

The Impulsive Child inevitably runs into conflicts with people in positions of authority. He becomes frustrated and angry when he can't have his way, and experiences limits as unfair, arbitrary, or punitive. For example, on one occasion during his incarceration, Tom demanded to be allowed to mail a package to his attorney. When told by his social worker that he would have to wait until the following day because the day's mail had already been picked up, he became enraged, insisting that the package had to be sent immediately because of an urgent deadline. Sensing that his argument was getting him nowhere, he went to a second social worker, and then to a third, each of whom reminded the patient that outgoing mail had to be sent before 12 noon, a rule that the patient knew quite well. Finally, Tom walked away in anger, saying that he would find some other way to solve the problem.

Patients with an Impulsive Child mode often grow up in families that lack firm and consistent limit setting. Such families may be overly indulgent, chaotic, or neglectful, and are usually lacking in parental supervision and control. For example, Tom had grown up in a wealthy family in which all of his desires were indulged. From an early age, he had developed behavior problems and was eventually diagnosed with attention deficit hyperactivity disorder. Tom's parents had always bailed him out of trouble, which reinforced a pattern in which Tom felt that he could get away with anything. Even during his forensic hospital stay, the parents had paid for a second psychiatric evaluation (which found that Tom had no psychiatric problems), and were trying to have him transferred to another facility where they were friends with the director. Thus, Tom's parents had given him the explicit and implicit message that all of his needs should be immediately gratified, and that he would never need to face the consequences of his actions. As a result, he developed an Impulsive Child mode that demanded that others immediately accede to his demands and became enraged, flipping into Angry Child mode, when others attempted to enforce limits.

# 11

## Maladaptive coping modes

Schema Therapy distinguishes three types of maladaptive coping modes: the Detached Protector, the Compliant Surrenderer, and the Overcompensator modes (Young et al., 2003). These modes correspond to the maladaptive coping styles of schema avoidance, surrender, and overcompensation, respectively. In contrast to the coping styles, however, which focus solely on coping behaviors, the coping modes are emotional states that involve emotions, cognitions, and behavioral responses that are active at a given moment, when early maladaptive schemas have been triggered.

The Detached Protector is a state of emotional avoidance. When in this state, patients deny feelings and problems, are emotionally detached, distant, and numb, or are intellectualized and super-rational. It may seem contradictory to refer to the Detached Protector as an emotional state, because it appears to involve an absence of emotion. However, it is more accurate to say that the Detached Protector involves active, albeit unconscious and automatic, efforts to keep emotions at a distance, resulting in a state of emotional numbness.

The Compliant Surrenderer mode is a state of compliance. It involves attempts to conform to others' expectations or demands, often at the expense of one's own needs. When in this state, patients act in accordance with their schemas, which may involve behaving passively, helplessly, or in a submissive manner.

The Overcompensator mode refers to a number of specific emotional states, which all involve overcompensatory forms of coping. Perhaps the prototypical Overcompensator mode is the Self-aggrandizer, which involves feelings of arrogance, superiority, and devaluation of others. When in the Self-aggrandizer mode, patients take a dominant "one-up" position over others, in an attempt to deny or make up for feelings of inferiority or deprivation.

While Young and colleagues (2003) posited three broad categories of maladaptive coping modes, it is possible to identify a variety of subcategories within them. For example, several variations on the Detached Protector mode have been identified. The Detached Self-soother mode involves attempts to calm or soothe one's feelings through compulsive, repetitive, or addictive behaviors, such as drug or alcohol use, binge eating, compulsive shopping, compulsive gambling, or internet addiction. When in this state, patients feel a pleasant sense of buzz, high, or numbness, which serves to block out painful feelings. In this detached state, time passes without being noticed and problems are temporarily forgotten.

In the Detached Self-stimulator mode, patients pursue sensations and thrills, and take risks, culminating in a state of excitement that also serves to avoid painful emotions. For example, such patients may pursue extreme sports, drive at high speeds, or engage in other dangerous pursuits, as if addicted to the risk itself.

Young et al. (2003) hypothesized that the Detached Self-soother and Self-stimulator modes play an important role in narcissistic personality disorder, by "filling up" the narcissist's sense of inner emptiness and loneliness. They also have an obvious connection to addictive disorders, operating according to a mechanism similar to the "self-medication" model of addiction (Khantzian, 1997) that posits that drug and alcohol use serve to quell painful emotions. It is important to note that some substances (e.g., heroin) may have a self-soothing function, while others (e.g., cocaine) are self-stimulating.

The Compliant Surrenderer mode involves passive, compliant, or dependent behaviors enacted in an attempt to avoid being mistreated by others. This mode is illustrated with the case of Drago. Drago grew up in a country where his ethnic group faced strong discrimination. From a young age, he was taught by his father that behaving in a deferential, subservient manner was the key to his survival. Even when harassed or bullied, Drago showed no visible signs of anger. Instead, he averted his eyes, slumped his shoulders, and spoke softly, seeking to placate his tormentors. He entered therapy after hitting his girlfriend in a rare moment of anger. In the preceding months, Drago had grown increasingly frustrated in the relationship. He had done everything possible to please his girlfriend: buying her presents, cooking her dinners, and giving in to her every whim. She, in turn, was critical and belittling towards him, complaining that he was weak and passive, and that he didn't earn enough money. One day, after suppressing his anger one time too many, he struck her.

In therapy sessions, Drago was nearly always in Compliant Surrenderer mode. He was invariably polite and cooperative. He agreed with all of his therapist's comments and tried his best to comply with her suggestions. He denied being angry, even on an occasion when his therapist accidently missed his appointment. He often wanted to know if he was being a "good patient." Eventually, after many months in Schema Therapy, he recognized the terrible price he had paid for his compliance and began learning to assert his needs and rights.

Overcompensator modes involve doing the opposite of schemas, in an attempt to escape from the painful emotions associated with them. Overcompensator modes involve a variety of specific emotional states, each characterized by a different form of overcompensation. For example, some individuals act in a superior, devaluing manner towards others, to avoid feeling inferior or insignificant (Self-aggrandizer mode). Others use bullying and aggression to overcome feelings of weakness or powerlessness (Bully and Attack mode). Yet others engage in obsessive or compulsive attempts to exercise order and control, to avoid feelings of helplessness (Obsessive Over-controller mode). When these modes are triggered, individuals flip into an emotional state that is the opposite of their schemas: feeling powerful rather than powerless; aggressive rather than weak; in control rather than helpless, respectively. By flipping into overcompensator modes, they escape from the painful feelings that arise when their schemas are triggered. As described later (see Point 26), an understanding of overcompensatory modes is essential in working with patients with narcissistic and antisocial personality disorders.

# 12

## Internalized parent modes

The two internalized parent modes are the Punitive Parent and the Demanding Parent. These modes have in common an internalized parental "voice" that criticizes or denigrates the patient (Punitive Parent) or places almost impossible demands on him (Demanding or Critical Parent). When in one of these modes, patients feel as if they are being scolded or berated, told that they are worthless and useless, that they are "screw-ups." In some cases, this internalized voice can be cruel or even abusive, telling one patient, for example, that it would have been better if she had never been born, or telling another that he is evil and that he deserves to die.

In Schema Therapy, these modes are thought to be based on patients' memories of actual criticism, punishment, or abuse by their parents or other caregivers. This does not mean that Schema Therapy views the Punitive/Critical mode as an exact representation of the patient's actual parents. Mental representations, as well as memories in general, are susceptible to a variety of possible distorting influences, such as emotional state effects and the degradation of memories over time (Brewin, Andrews, & Gotlib, 1993). Nevertheless, Schema Therapy views these representations of negative parental behaviors as largely accurate reflections of the child's reality, a view that is consistent with research that indicates that traumatic memories are usually accurately remembered in their central details (i.e., the core features of the abuse), whereas peripheral details may involve some distortion or inaccuracy (Brewin et al., 1993).

The Punitive Parent mode can be particularly severe in patients with borderline personality disorder. When in Punitive Parent mode, patients with this disorder experience a degree of self-punishment that can feel unbearable and provoke suicidal behavior or self-injury. In such states, the borderline patient flips back and forth between the side of herself that berates herself for real or imagined faults or transgressions (Punitive Parent mode) and the side that experiences the intense inner pain of a child that is being punished (Vulnerable Child mode). Thus, the Punitive/Critical Parent mode and the Vulnerable Child mode exist in an abuser–victim relationship to one another, with the critical, punitive voices triggering painful feelings of worthlessness and depression.

The Demanding Parent mode is the side of the patient that places almost impossible demands on him. This often takes the form of demands for achievement or success, but can also involve other types of demands, for example, a demand that a child sacrifice his own autonomy to take care of the parent. The Demanding Parent mode bears an obvious connection to the Unrelenting Standards schema, which involves perfectionistic standards that are impossible to reach. When in Demanding Parent mode, the patient experiences unrelenting pressure to push himself to succeed. Patients with this mode often believe that they need this side of themselves to push them to achieve, and fail to recognize the way in which this side can be crippling.

Susan, a patient with a strong Demanding Parent mode, had spent months fruitlessly trying to write her first novel. She diligently set aside time every day to write, but nothing she wrote was good enough to meet up to her standards. She pushed and pushed herself, but always found her writing to be inferior. Only greatness would satisfy her. After editing and re-editing her writing for hours, she would eventually throw it away in frustration, only to start the process again the next day, with the same outcome. Like many patients with a Demanding Parent mode, she had always believed that she needed to push herself relentlessly to succeed. At the same time, this side of her felt like a burden that she couldn't escape. As a child, she had been regarded as a genius by her father, who had pushed her to read literary works that were clearly above her head, but which she dutifully read anyway. She believed that she was destined to become a great woman of letters. The eventual realization that she was a good, but not great, writer was intolerable. To her, the only alternative to greatness was mediocrity.

After suffering through many months of writer's block, Susan entered Schema Therapy. She learned to speak back to her Demanding Parent side, and to affirm that the Little Child within her had worth and deserved love and attention, even if she wasn't a genius. With this realization, she was able to resume writing. Like many patients with Demanding Parent mode, Susan had a parent who had valued achievement above all else. Such parents often push their children to fulfill their own unrealized ambitions or unfulfilled needs. Her father had been an intellectual who had never achieved his dreams of an academic career. He had transferred these dreams to his daughter, pushing her relentlessly to achieve them. Thus, the driven, never satisfied quality of the Demanding Parent mode can reflect the frustrated strivings of a parent who uses his child to fulfill his own frustrated needs.

# 13

## Healthy modes: Healthy Adult, Contented Child

Earlier, we explained that the Vulnerable Child mode is often the focus of therapy and that access to it is a key part of the healing process. Another key part of the process involves the strengthening of the two healthy modes – the Healthy Adult and the Contented Child.

### *Healthy Adult mode*

The Healthy Adult mode is the part of the self that is capable, strong, and well-functioning. It includes those functional cognitions and behaviors that are needed to carry out appropriate adult functions such as working, parenting, taking responsibility, and committing to both people and actions. This part of the self is also the one that pursues pleasurable adult activities such as intellectual, aesthetic, and cultural interests, sex, health maintenance, and athletic activities.

The therapist forms an alliance with the Healthy Adult mode. In many cases, when this mode is relatively weak, the therapist also serves as a model for its emergence. Most adult patients have some version of this mode, but they vary drastically in how effective it is. Healthier, higher-functioning patients have a stronger Healthy Adult mode; more severely symptomatic patients usually have a weaker Healthy Adult mode. Borderline patients often have almost no Healthy Adult mode, so with them the therapist is augmenting or helping to create a mode that is extremely undeveloped.

The Healthy Adult mode, like an internalized therapist, has to respond flexibly to the various other modes. It nurtures, protects, and validates the Vulnerable Child mode, sets limits on the impulsivity and the angry outbursts of the Angry and Impulsive Child modes, and combats the effects of maladaptive coping modes and dysfunctional parent modes. For example, when psychologically healthy people face frustrations, they have a Healthy Adult mode that can usually keep angry emotions and behaviors from going out of control. In contrast, borderline patients typically have a very weak Healthy Adult mode. When they face similar frustrations, their "Angry Child" mode is triggered without any substantial counterbalancing force. In the absence of a strong Healthy Adult mode, anger can completely take over.

In the course of treatment, patients internalize the therapist's behavior as part of their own Healthy Adult mode. Initially, the therapist serves as the Healthy Adult whenever the patient is incapable of doing so. For example, in the early stages of therapy, if the patient is unable to combat the Punitive Parent on his own, the therapist will intervene. However, as the patient begins to develop the ability to battle the Punitive Parent on his own, the therapist steps back, intervening less often or not at all.

It is important (but sometimes difficult) not to confuse the Detached Protector mode and the Healthy Adult mode. At times, a patient who is detached can come across as rational, functioning, and in control, and the therapist may mistakenly support these behaviors when in fact they should be counteracted. What helps distinguish a bona fide Healthy Adult mode from the false health that characterizes a Detached Protector mode is that the former involves a genuine experience of the full range of emotions, while the latter usually involves restriction of emotion and affect. As a consequence, being in a Healthy Adult mode allows patients to engage and acknowledge all of their myriad feelings, while being in a Detached Protector mode leads them to deny or invalidate certain parts, especially the Vulnerable Child mode and its neediness.

### Contented Child mode

A second and related adaptive mode is the Contented Child. When in this mode, people feel at peace because their core emotional needs are currently met. They experience others as loving and appropriately protective, and they feel connected to them, nurtured, and validated. Because of this sense of security, they feel fulfilled, worthwhile, and self-confident, and are able to have a sense of optimism, spontaneity, and contentment.

As is true with other child modes, every child is born with the innate capacity to experience contentment. The degree to which it is actually experienced depends on the frequency and regularity with which childhood needs are adequately met. In a sense, then, the Contented Child mode develops in the absence of considerable deprivation, and therefore in the absence of considerable schema activation.

The Contented Child mode represents the capacity to experience and express spontaneity, glee, and playful happiness. In its original form (i.e., in children), it is a care-free mode, but its existence requires much care, either from external adults (parents) or from one's own Healthy Adult mode. If the Healthy Adult is strong and functioning, it creates the freedom necessary for the Contented Child to thrive.

14

## Limited reparenting

Schema Therapy involves two fundamental therapeutic stances – *limited reparenting* and *empathic confrontation*. We devote the next two Points to these concepts.

The central project of Schema Therapy is to help adults get their own emotional needs met, even when these needs may have never been met in the past. To achieve that, the therapy relationship itself needs to be one in which the patient's needs are recognized, articulated, validated, and – within certain boundaries – fulfilled. The most important fulfillment is of those needs that were not met by the patients' parents when they were children. We refer to this bounded fulfillment of needs as *limited reparenting*.

Which needs are fulfilled in a given therapy relationship depends to a large degree on the schemas or modes most active for that patient. For example, a patient with strong Abandonment and Mistrust/Abuse schemas (and with an unmet need for safety and stability) will most benefit from a therapist's emphasis on constancy, reliability, honesty, and availability. Another patient, who has the schema of Unrelenting Standards or a strong Critical Parent mode, will gain the most from a therapist who is generous with (authentic) praise and acceptance.

Through limited reparenting, the therapist supplies patients with a partial antidote to needs that were not adequately met in childhood. This concept is similar to the one of *corrective emotional experience* (Alexander & French, 1946), but in this context refers to actions specifically designed to counteract the patient's early maladaptive schemas.

Limited reparenting requires assessing the specific reparenting needs of the patients. There is a variety of ways to do this:

the therapist can gather information from childhood history, from reports of interpersonal difficulties, from questionnaires, and from imagery exercises. Often, the best source of information is attending to the relationship itself, and to events within that relationship. All of these shed light on patients' schemas and coping styles, and suggest the specific reparenting needs.

Many of the ideal qualities of schema therapists are the ones that allow for effective limited reparenting. Maybe the most important one is flexibility: the therapist needs to continuously attend to and assess the patient's reparenting needs. At times, the reparenting needs will call for a strong emphasis on trust, stability, and emotional nurturance. At other times they may call for an emphasis on independence, or on the freedom to be playful and creative. In a way, the therapist should be like a good parent with the flexible capacity to meet the patient's (or the child's) needs.

Other qualities that facilitate limited reparenting are the capacity to tolerate and contain strong affect, the ability to be validating and warm, and the skill to maintain realistic expectations and appropriate boundaries. It is important to note that schema therapists extend typical therapy boundaries – by encouraging out-of-session contact, using (judicious) self-disclosure, and expressing genuine warmth and care. This extension of the boundaries is done to permit the relationship to become similar to a parental, caring relationship. Nonetheless, schema therapists are careful not to violate boundaries in ways that would be damaging to patients.

Through limited reparenting, the schema therapist provides the patient with a fulfillment of needs and the patient gradually learns to accept the therapist as a stable object. With time, the kind of warmth and caring associated with that object is internalized and becomes part of the patient's own Healthy Adult mode. A serious challenge for therapists is to determine which needs can be met by the patients themselves, and which stand to benefit from the therapist's reparenting. As a rule, reparenting is done only when the therapist sees needs that went unmet in the patient's early development, and that (without intervention) would continue to go unmet. Initially, the therapist serves as the Healthy Adult whenever the patient is incapable of doing so. For example, if the patient is able to battle the Punitive Parent on his own, the therapist does not intervene. However, if the patient is unable to battle the Punitive Parent and instead attacks himself endlessly without defending himself, then the therapist intervenes and battles the Punitive Parent for the patient. Gradually the patient takes over the Healthy Adult role.

Schema therapists take great pains to provide limited reparenting in a caring and respectful way, rather than in a condescending one. At the same time, patients' core needs are seen as essential and universal requirements and not as frivolous fantasies; their fulfillment is therefore quite different from sheer gratification. When done correctly, limited reparenting can easily be immune to two critiques of this therapeutic stance: that it is paternalistic or denigrating to the patient, or that it is a form of counterproductive gratification of the patient's fantasies.

Since the therapist can only provide the patient with "limited" reparenting, it is inevitable that there will be a gulf between what the patient wants and what the therapist can give. Rather then using impersonal explanations of limits (i.e., "It is the policy of our center to prohibit any behavior that might lead to suicide"), the therapist communicates in a personal manner (i.e., "For the sake of my own peace of mind, I have to know that you're safe").

# 15

## Empathic confrontation

Empathic confrontation, along with limited reparenting, is one of the two central "pillars" of the Schema Therapy treatment approach (Young et al., 2003). In empathic confrontation, the therapist confronts the patient on his maladaptive behaviors and cognitions, but in an empathic, non-judgmental way. This technique only works if the therapist has genuine compassion for the patient. That is, he is able to empathize with the reasons for which the patient engages in these behaviors, but at the same time emphasizes the self-defeating nature of these responses and the necessity of changing them. The Schema Therapy language of schemas, coping responses, and modes facilitates empathic confrontation by giving the therapist and patient a common set of concepts and vocabulary with which to understand the patient's maladaptive attempts at coping. These concepts are morally and emotionally neutral, in that they view maladaptive behavior as a consequence of self-defeating patterns rather than as stemming from moral flaws.

Empathic confrontation can be used to confront the patient with his self-defeating behavior outside or inside of the therapy session. A therapist's in-session empathic confrontation can be extremely powerful because it gives both parties the chance to examine the patient's behavior as it is occurring in the "here-and-now" of the therapy relationship. This enables the therapist to demonstrate to the patient the obstacles being put in the way of intimacy and of getting the patient's emotional needs met.

Empathic confrontation can be done either with the original Schema Therapy language of schemas and coping responses, or with the more elaborate language of modes and mode work.

We illustrate both with the example of Robert, a young man who had been physically and emotionally abused as a child, got into frequent heated arguments with his boss. It is easy to empathise with the reasons that the patient got into these conflicts. Because of the way Robert had been mistreated as a child, he expected that other people were out to hurt or humiliate him (Mistrust/Abuse and Defectiveness/Shame schemas), and had similar expectations towards his boss.

When Robert was young, fighting back against his parents was his only way of combating their abuse and preserving his self-respect (an overcompensating coping response). It was natural for Robert to fight back against his boss, who was also experienced as abusive. However, because Robert's reactions were rooted in the past, they often went too far. His attempts to protect himself were experienced by others as extreme and out of proportion. As a result, not only did others fail to understand his legitimate grievances, they saw him as angry and out of control.

The therapist used the concepts of schemas and coping responses, which Robert had already learned in Schema Therapy, to confront this self-defeating behavior. By framing the conflict with his boss in terms of schemas and coping responses, the therapist was able to empathize with the reasons for Robert's behavior in a caring and non-judgmental way, while at the same time pointing out their self-defeating consequences. This approach enabled Robert to view his interactions with his boss in more realistic and less schema-driven terms, and to adopt a less confrontational style in these interactions.

Were the therapist to use mode language, the basic approach to empathic confrontation would remain the same. However, terms like "the abused child side of you," and "the angry child side," would be substituted for schemas or coping responses. For example, the therapist may say:

> "When your boss criticizes you there is a side of you, the 'Abused Child' side, which feels that he is being abused all

over again, just like you were by your parents. It's no surprise that you become angry, and turn the tables on your boss by going on the attack. When you were a child, fighting back was the only way that you could preserve your self-respect. However, when you get into a fight with your boss now, he doesn't see the side of you that feels abused or mistreated. He just sees the 'Angry Child' side and feels attacked. As a result, you don't get what you need, which is empathy and understanding. That's what you want from your boss; it's what you really needed from your parents, too."

# Part 2

# PRACTICAL POINTS

# 16

## The assessment process: Focused life history interview, schema inventories, and self-monitoring

The second half of this book discusses the practical application of Schema Therapy. We begin (Points 16–19) by discussing the assessment and conceptualization process which sets the stage for this application.

Schema therapists begin their work with patients with a comprehensive assessment process. The process usually involves several sessions (typically 2–4) devoted to gathering information in a variety of assessment methods. The broad goals of the assessment process are:

(a) To learn about the dysfunctional life patterns present in the patient's life
(b) To identify the early maladaptive schemas, coping styles, and predominant modes that play a part in creating or maintaining these life patterns
(c) To learn about the developmental origins of the schemas, coping styles, and modes
(d) To assess the patient's temperament, and learn about ways in which this temperament may have interacted with other developmental factors (e.g., deprivation, trauma, or over-indulgence; see Point 2).

The remainder of this Point describes three of the methods used to attain these goals: the focused life history interview, the employment of self-report inventories, and the use of self-monitoring. Point 17 reviews the use of guided imagery for assessment, and Point 18 discusses the information gleaned from the emerging therapy relationship itself. Importantly, none of these sources of data holds a privileged position compared with the others. Instead, the therapist's role is to use all of these data to generate clinical hypotheses, and to adjust these hypotheses as more data are collected until an integrated understanding emerges. This assessment and integration process culminates in a written case conceptualization, which is shared with the patient (Point 19). The case conceptualization spells out both current problems and patterns as well as possible developmental origins for these problems, and frames all of these using the concepts of Schema Therapy (i.e., needs, schemas, coping responses, and modes). We share the conceptualization with patients for two main purposes: first, it allows the therapist and the patient to collaboratively hone and refine their joint understanding. Second, it helps educate the patient about Schema Therapy.

### *Initial evaluation and focused life history*

In the first session (or first several sessions) of Schema Therapy, therapists interview patients to learn about their presenting problems, their goals for therapy, and their unmet emotional needs. Clarifying what these problems and goals are, and keeping them in focus, ensures that the patient's agenda in seeking therapy continues to guide the therapy process. Without this clarification, the therapy carries the risk of drifting in focus, as often happens in some insight-oriented and supportive therapies. In this regard, Schema Therapy continues to resemble CBT, though the problems and goals addressed in Schema Therapy are usually broader or more pervasive than those in more time-limited CBT treatments for Axis I problems. Nonetheless, like other CBT therapists, schema therapists strive to define problems and goals in specific terms and not in vague generalities. For example, instead of referring to "the patient's relationship problems," the therapist would hypothesize that "the patient repeatedly engages in a demand–withdraw cycle with her partner, feels rejected, and reacts strongly to such signs of rejection."

The suitability of Schema Therapy for the patient's needs is also determined at this stage. Schema Therapy is not always indicated, and at times, may be more suitable at a later stage of therapy after acute Axis I symptoms have been addressed with other evidence-based approaches (see Point 28). In particular, the following situations would indicate that Schema Therapy may not be the right choice:

(a) The presence of acute and relatively severe symptoms of an Axis I disorder that are currently untreated and that could be better treated by the focused application of an appropriate treatment (e.g., medication or a focused CBT protocol for addressing an anxiety disorder).
(b) The presence of an acute major crisis (though for some patients with a life pattern of recurrent crises, Schema Therapy should be considered).
(c) The presence of psychosis (though transient psychotic symptoms, sometimes present in borderline personality disorder, are not a contraindication for Schema Therapy).
(d) Current alcohol or drug abuse that is of sufficient severity to interfere with the conduct of therapy.
(e) Presenting problems that are situational and do not seem to stem from long-standing schemas, coping styles, or prominent maladaptive modes.

These are not hard-and-fast exclusion rules for Schema Therapy. In fact, Schema Therapy has been applied successfully for patients for whom chronic Axis I problems (e.g., depression or substance abuse) were the main concern, and where previous attempts at intervention were met with relapse or with lack of success. However, some patients may benefit from beginning therapy with a narrower focus (e.g., addressing anxiety or mood symptoms) and later transitioning into Schema Therapy.

When schema therapists interview patients about their history, they are trying to determine whether the presenting problems reflect long-standing patterns in the patient's life, or are constrained to a narrower context. When problems do seem to reflect schema activation, the therapist works to identify previous periods of such activation. This can help clarify which triggers exert the greatest influence on the patient, as well as which thoughts, images, feelings, and behaviors occur when the schemas are activated. Similarly, the characteristic coping styles and predominant modes that emerge in these charged situations can be noted.

To augment the information gathered in the interview, therapists may ask patients to complete one or more self-report inventories as homework. Patients return these inventories in the next session and review their answers with the therapist. Several inventories have been developed and are used for assessing schemas, coping responses, predominant modes, and developmental history. (For a complete list and updated versions of these instruments, as well as information about their availability in various languages, see www.schematherapy.com/ or www.isst-online.com/)

## *Young Schema Questionnaire*

The most widely used questionnaire is the Young Schema Questionnaire (YSQ), now in its third edition. Patients typically complete this questionnaire between the first and second sessions (though some therapists have patients complete it before beginning therapy and others may choose to delay its use, especially with more reserved or suspicious patients). The YSQ contains items reflective of 18 schemas (see Point 3 for the schema listing), each rated on a 1–6 scale anchored by "completely untrue of me" and "describes me perfectly." Clinically, we have found that counting only extreme scores (4s, 5s, and 6s) helps identify the most prominent schemas, though others have argued that a regular averaging of all scores for each schema works better.

In addition to using the YSQ as a normed test yielding a simple "profile" of high- and low-scoring schemas, we have found it useful to use it as a springboard for discussion. The information provided in it serves as prompts for querying the patient more about symptoms or behaviors they endorsed. For example, we may ask patients to tell us more about how a particular, highly-rated statement, relates to their life. After asking about two or more related items, we may use the opportunity to note to patients both the name of the schema and its possible relevance to their life (by suggesting a reading from the patient-focused *Reinventing your life* (Young & Klosko, 1993), or by pointing to the description of the relevant schema in a handout).

Patients' responses on the YSQ may agree or disagree with impressions developed by the therapist from other parts of the assessment process (e.g., the life history or the imagery for assessment). When discrepancies occur, the therapist tries to clarify them to determine which source of information provides more valid data – in other words, which "feels right" to both the patient and the therapist. In any case, the most useful information usually emerges not from the answers or scores themselves, but from the conversation that ensues when the therapist and the patient review the questionnaire together.

Some patients struggle with completing the YSQ. Rather than insisting that it (or any other questionnaire) be completed, the therapist would explore the reasons for such balking, and may forgo using the questionnaire. As we note in Point 18, such reactions are often quite informative in their own right regarding the patient's schemas and coping styles. Additionally, with certain patients (see Point 25), we deliberately refrain from using the YSQ.

## *Other inventories and self-report questionnaires*

A second, and also widely used, inventory is the Young Parenting Inventory (YPI). Like the YSQ, the YPI includes items rated on a 1–6 scale and is organized according to childhood experiences that are thought to be possible origins for specific schemas. The YPI is shorter, though each item is rated twice – once for each parental figure. As with the YSQ, we use the YPI as a source of clinical hypotheses rather than a normed instrument.

At times, patients find it easier to complete the YPI than the YSQ. This could be due to its brevity, to its focus on the past, or to the objective nature of many of its questions (in contrast to the subjective nature of most YSQ questions). Nonetheless, the same considerations that apply to the YSQ (i.e., querying discrepancies, using the instrument as a springboard for discussion, and handling difficulties experienced while completing it) apply here as well.

Several additional instruments (the Young-Rygh Avoidance Inventory, the Young Compensation Inventory, and the Schema Mode Inventory) have been developed and are in use to assess coping styles or predominant modes. In addition, many schema therapists have found it useful to assign Lazarus and Lazarus's (1991) very comprehensive Multimodal Life History Inventory, which queries widely about behaviors, affect, sensations, imagery, cognitions, interpersonal relationships, and drugs/biology (i.e., the BASIC-ID). Other symptom scales (e.g., the Beck Depression Inventory) are often used at intake and at later points to determine symptom change.

### *Self-monitoring as an assessment tool*

Self-monitoring of daily events and of the thoughts, feelings, and behaviors that arise in response to these events are frequently used in various CBT approaches, and can be of great use in Schema Therapy as well – above and beyond their use as a cognitive intervention (see Point 21). Specifically, schema therapists may ask patients to begin completing schema diaries (described in Point 21), or more rudimentary self-monitoring event logs (such as the daily thought record form depicted in Figure 21.1 on page 106) on a daily basis starting with the first session. By the third or fourth session, multiple records are available to review and will often reveal important diagnostic information. Though the daily records do not require the patient to identify the schema by name, they help document the operation of the schema and its effects. For example, a patient with a strong Abandonment schema may report multiple instances of interpersonal rejection, coupled with thoughts, feelings, and behaviors that are consistent with this schema.

More importantly, these daily records provide both the therapist and the patient with potent examples from everyday life. In this way, they complement the historical information obtained in the interview and the generalized impressions provided by self-report questionnaires. As therapists integrate these various sources of information (along with those obtained from guided imagery (Point 17) and from the therapy relationship itself (Point 18)), the specific details obtained from daily records help make the conceptualization real and detailed for the patient.

# 17

## The assessment process: Guided imagery

Guided imagery is a technique in which the therapist asks the patient to visualize a certain scene, experience, or episode. It is a key experiential technique in Schema Therapy, and is widely used in the later change phase of the therapy (see Point 22). However, imagery is often also an indispensable part of the assessment process.

As an assessment tool, imagery is used to trigger the patient's schemas in the therapy session so that both the therapist and the patient can feel them; it complements other forms of assessment (including the interview and inventories) by moving the discussion of schemas from "cold" to "hot" cognitions.

Imagery for assessment is usually introduced within the first 5–6 sessions – that is, relatively early in the assessment and education phase. When used for the first time, imagery usually requires devoting close to an entire session, with ample time for preparation and debriefing, as well as for the imagery exercise itself. Sometimes patients are distraught after an imagery session. Starting imagery work early in the session helps ensure that there is enough time for patients to recover before they have to leave.

When patients are afraid of the imagery work, the therapist attempts to set them at ease by reminding them that they are in control of the imagery. Thus, although the therapist may invite them to close their eyes to enhance their concentration, they may open their eyes if they become overwhelmed. Because of traumatic histories, feelings of mistrust, or anxiety, some patients participate in imagery exercises with downcast, rather than closed, eyes or request that the therapist not watch them during the exercises. Therapists make these necessary accommodations. After the exercise, the therapist may need to "ground" these patients in the present moment before the session ends using a mindfulness exercise. With later repeated uses of imagery, patients tend to become less apprehensive about it and less time may be necessary, though we still make sure to begin imagery early in a session.

Before engaging the patient in an imagery exercise, the therapist presents the rationale for the use of imagery, which includes three objectives:

(1) Identifying and triggering the patient's schemas
(2) Understanding the childhood origins of the schemas
(3) Linking schemas to presenting problems.

In the imagery exercise, patients close their eyes and let an image float to the top of their minds. We ask them not to force the image, but to let it come on its own. Once patients get an image, we ask them to describe it to us, out loud and in the present tense. We help them make it vivid and emotionally real. One guiding principle is to give the least amount of instruction necessary for the patient to produce a workable image. We want the images that patients produce to be entirely their own; therefore we avoid making suggestions or giving many prompts. Thus, we avoid inserting the therapist's own ideas or hypotheses. The goal is to elicit core images – those connected with primary emotions such as fear, rage, shame, and grief, that are linked to the patients' early maladaptive schemas and childhood histories.

Schema therapists encourage patients to use pictures for the image, not just words or thoughts: "Imagery is not like thinking or free association – it's more like watching a movie. I want you to experience it, to become immersed in it, be a part of the movie and live through all the events that unfold." The suggestion to speak in the first person and in the present tense is done for the same purpose – to allow the patient to become absorbed in the image.

In the assessment imagery (and, for some patients, in most or all subsequent imagery exercises), we begin and end the imagery with a safe place. This is done for two purposes. First, it allows the patient to practice becoming immersed in an image in a non-threatening way. Second, it provides refuge when the imagery material has been particularly upsetting. If patients are unable to generate a safe place, the therapist devotes sufficient time to help them construct such an image. For many people, beautiful natural scenes work well; for some, the only safe place may be the therapy office itself.

Once patients are able to fully experience the "safe place" image, we ask them to get an image of an upsetting childhood situation with one of their parents, or with any other significant figure from their childhood or adolescence. We instruct them to speak to these people in their images, expressing what they are thinking and feeling, and what they wish they could get from the other person. We ask them to imagine (out loud) the other person's response, and to carry on a dialogue between themselves (as children) and the other (parental) figure. We then ask patients to switch to an image from their current life that feels the same as the childhood situation. Once again, the patient carries on a dialogue with the person from their adult life, saying aloud what they are thinking and feeling, and what they wish they could get from the other person.

To elicit schemas and modes that may be tied only to one particular parent (but not to the other parent), we repeat the assessment imagery exercise with reference to each parent (and to other significant figures from the patient's childhood or adolescence). This usually requires devoting several sessions to this part of the assessment process, though we tend not to conduct two imagery sessions back-to-back but instead alternate them with sessions devoted to other forms of assessment or to the establishment of rapport.

The typical sequence of imagery exercises begins with an upsetting image from childhood and proceeds to an upsetting image from current life, reinforcing one of the central goals, which is the recognition of the childhood origins of unmet needs and early maladaptive schemas. This sequence, however, is not set in stone. For example, if a patient enters a session already upset about a current situation, we can use an image of this situation as the starting place and then work back in time, asking the patient to get an image from childhood that feels the same. We can use an image of a specific symptom in the patient's body, or a strong but not well understood emotion, as starting places. For example, we might say, "Can you get an image of your back when you're in pain? What does it look like? What is the pain saying?"

Conducting imagery exercises requires great care and is often met with some difficulty on the patient's part. If a patient balks at the idea of imagery or reports being unable to generate an image, we address these reactions as examples of the (maladaptive) avoidant coping style or the Detached Protector mode. For brevity's sake, we will simply list several of the steps we follow in overcoming such avoidance:

(1) Educating the patient about the rationale for imagery work
(2) Examining the pros and cons of doing the exercise (often using another experiential technique borrowed from Gestalt Therapy – the two-chair approach)
(3) Starting with soothing imagery and only gradually introducing more anxiety-provoking material
(4) Using affect regulation techniques such as mindfulness or relaxation training
(5) Exploring the use of psychotropic medication to reduce anxiety.

# 18

## The assessment process: In-session behaviors and the therapy relationship

A patient's unmet needs, schemas, coping behaviors, and modes are often present in the therapy relationship, and the assessment process therefore includes considerable attention to the therapy relationship as a source of information. Schemas, by their nature, produce characteristic behaviors across situations and relationships. For example, an individual with a strong Approval-seeking schema will come into a new situation with heightened awareness of the other person's reaction to her. Another patient with an Entitlement schema will enter any relationship with jarring demands for his partner. These characteristic behavioral, cognitive, and emotional patterns have a high chance of being triggered during the assessment phase: the personal nature of the therapist's questions, along with the uncertainty and novelty that are common in early stages of therapy, naturally "provide" many opportunities for such triggering.

First, patients react in schema-driven ways to the therapeutic relationship. For example, a patient with an Approval-seeking schema may minimize their problems or act in an overly compliant way to gain approval; one with an Entitlement schema may demand unreasonable special accommodations such as excessive flexibility with session timing and length; a patient with a Mistrust/Abuse schema may show great concern for confidentiality and may feel uncomfortable with the therapist's note-taking; and one with an Abandonment schema may resist the emotional connection for fear of being abandoned by the therapist once trust is established. (Note that the inverse is also true: therapists' schemas get triggered as well, an issue we explore in Point 30.)

Beyond the novelty of the relationship itself, the tools used in the assessment phase often trigger schemas because of their strongly personal nature. For example, when assigned the extensive YSQ or the Multimodal Inventory to complete, a patient with a Dependence schema may request extensive help; when the rationale for conducting imagery for assessment is introduced, a patient with a Failure schema may express reluctance to even try the imagery, for fear of not being able to do imagery well enough.

When schemas become triggered in-session or in reaction to the therapist, the therapist and the patient can discuss what transpired, and can work collaboratively to identify and name both the schemas themselves and the specific events that triggered them. Because this all happens in the therapy room, the feelings, thoughts, and behaviors are vividly present, which increases both the confidence with which they can be recognized and the clarity with which they can be conveyed to the patient. To demonstrate that these reactions are indeed schema-driven, the therapist will ask the patient to remember other situations in which they have felt and acted in these ways, as well as other people who have elicited such reactions from them in the past.

Some behaviors and reactions that are observed in-session may reflect schema modes (i.e., temporary states) more than chronic schemas themselves. A common example involves patients appearing distant or calm even as they retell very upsetting life histories. Schema therapists recognize this as the behavior of a coping mode (namely, the Avoidant or Detached Protector mode) and make a note of this, as well as of other modes that are evident in the patients' presentation.

Attending to the relationship bears some resemblance to the psychoanalytic notion of transference. However, the therapeutic stance of schema therapists (particularly the limited reparenting stance, which guides the therapist from the first moment of therapy) strongly distinguishes their use of the therapy relationship as a source of information (and later, change) from psychoanalytic transference analysis. As we explain elsewhere

(Points 14 and 29), limited reparenting is decidedly different from therapeutic neutrality. Traditionally-trained therapists may worry that transference would be harder to interpret if the therapist is anything but neutral. We do not share this worry. Our experience (and that of others: e.g., Wachtel, 2007) suggests that even when the therapist's basic stance is a warm and nurturing (or "gratifying") one, it will elicit very different reactions from patients with differing schemas. These strongly-ingrained emotional responses remain very informative.

A final point about the use of the therapy relationship as a source of information: It goes without saying that the relationship continues to be of central importance beyond the assessment and education phase, and is a central vehicle for intervention in Schema Therapy (see, in particular, Points 14, 15, 23, and 29).

# 19

## Educating the patient about the schema and mode models, and using the schema case conceptualization form

The assessment phase culminates in a written and integrated conceptualization tying together the information gleaned from the interview, questionnaires, imagery for assessment, daily thought records, and from the therapist's attention to the therapy relationship and to in-session behaviors. Some of these sources of information are more detached and cerebral (e.g., self-report questionnaires) and others more emotionally charged (e.g., imagery for assessment). Together, they generate information that is both intellectual and emotional, which allows patients to both *understand* and *feel* their schemas. In this way, both patients and therapists can determine whether all parts of the conceptualization "fit" – that is, whether they resonate with the patient's emotional experience.

The culminating conceptualization (see Table 19.1) is similar to, but broader than, ones used in other CBT case formulation approaches (e.g., Persons, 2008). Like these approaches, it describes the patient's symptoms, disorders, and presenting problems; it proposes mechanisms both for the emergence and for the maintenance of the problems; it identifies present-day triggers for the problems; and it addresses the origins of the mechanisms. It expands on these approaches in several ways. First, it plainly identifies schemas, coping responses, and modes. Second, it draws specific attention to cognition (core cognitions and distortions), behavior (surrender, escape, or overcompensation), experience/imagery (core childhood memories), relational aspects (information about the therapy relationship), and possible temperamental/biological factors. Finally, it has the

**Table 19.1** Schema Therapy case conceptualization

1. Patient name, age, marital status, children (and ages), educational background, racial/ethnic/religious background, occupation, and overall level of functioning.
2. Axis I symptoms/diagnoses.
3. Current (presenting) problems, connecting them to longer-standing life patterns.
4. Developmental origin (with information about all caregivers and other relevant family members).
5. Core childhood images/memories.
6. Core unmet needs.
7. Relevant schemas.
8. Current triggers for these schemas.
9. Coping behaviors (including surrender, escape, and overcompensation behaviors, if present).
10. Relevant schema modes.
11. Possible temperamental/biological factors.
12. Core cognitions and distortions.
13. Information about the therapy relationship.
14. Goals and focus for change.

explicit goal of providing an integrative "story" about the origin, maintenance, and possible resolution of the patient's presenting problems.

The conceptualization is created collaboratively with the patient and is tailored to the patient. This process often spans more than one session. In most cases, the therapist presents the case conceptualization as a work-in-progress or a draft, and solicits the patient's feedback on it. The therapist explains the different elements of the conceptualization form, and offers their take on the patient's experience; the patient then provides additional information and has the opportunity to suggest changes or amendments to the draft. The terms used to denote particular schemas and modes are entirely flexible and can be replaced with terms that "make sense" for the patient. For example, rather than using the term "Detached Protector mode," the patient and the therapist may refer to "the bubble" or "the wall."

The Schema Therapy assessment and education phase usually occurs early in the therapy relationship. However, when the therapist determines that there are prominent Axis I symptoms that require clinical attention, or in cases in which the patient first presented explicitly for more focused evidence-based treatment, the therapist would first use conventional CBT techniques (or other evidence-based approaches). In such cases, the assessment and education phase can occur at a later point in the therapy. This will require a "changing of gears," which can be done at the request of the patient or at the suggestion of the therapist. We return to this in Point 28.

The case conceptualization serves as a guide for the therapy itself. It identifies the key targets for intervention: those schemas, coping responses, and modes that are keeping the patient from getting their needs met, and that require clinical attention. Arriving at a good conceptualization is therefore very important, as it sets the stage for effective and focused subsequent work. An accurate conceptualization also helps the patient feel validated and understood, and therefore strengthens the therapeutic alliance. Finally, both the conceptualization itself and the process through which it is created also serve a powerful educational purpose within the therapy. They provide a developmental account for the patient's presenting problems and difficulties in life. They offer a vocabulary for describing experiences that were often too difficult to articulate. And they suggest to the patient that there is a structure – to the current distress and to the way out of it.

In the course of the assessment phase, and particularly in the process of creating the conceptualization form, patients come to recognize their schemas and modes, and to understand the developmental origins of these schemas. They begin to see how these maladaptive patterns have recurred throughout their lives. And they start to see how maladaptive coping behaviors or pervasive coping styles, which developed to regulate their schemas, are often a product of both individual temperament and early life experiences. They link their schemas and modes to their presenting problems, and begin to view the continuity in experience (and often in symptoms) from childhood to the present.

The process of creating and reviewing the case conceptualization straddles the assessment and intervention phases of therapy. In most cases, it provides a striking example of how woven together those two phases usually are. First, the schema therapist begins adopting the therapeutic stances of limited reparenting and empathic confrontation from the initiation of therapy. Second, the therapist is guided by the knowledge that assessment and education are powerful interventions themselves, and are not just a "prelude" to intervention. Finally, assessment and education do not cease once the case conceptualization is completed. At all times during therapy, the therapist attends to new information and, when needed, revisits and redrafts the case conceptualization.

# 20

## Toolbox 1: Relational techniques

Schema Therapy is strongly relational and interpersonal. Schema therapists are not a neutral screen on which the patient can project – they are very actively present in the room. The particular type of presence distinguishes Schema Therapy from psychodynamic therapy on the one hand, but also from other schools of CBT on the other. This is because, unlike other cognitive behavioral therapists, schema therapists are guided by the ideas of limited reparenting and empathic confrontation.

The relational stance of the schema therapist (described in greater length in Points 14, 15, and 29) serves two goals. The first and overarching goal is to establish a caring, trusting relationship that allows the patient to undergo the corrective emotional experience of having their needs met in a sufficient, healthy, and adaptive way. A second goal is to use the relationship as a safe place for exploring interpersonal and behavioral cycles that are driven by the patient's schemas and modes, and that may otherwise go unnoticed (or at least occur without the opportunity to stop, examine, and learn from them). Doing so in a caring, nurturing, and non-punitive manner is, in a way, not just a goal, but also a means to achieving the corrective emotional experience that therapy tries to create.

Schema therapists attend to moments when schemas or coping styles are triggered in the therapy relationship itself – either in-session or outside of it (e.g., in the patient's response to homework assignments or in their use of out-of-session contact). Similarly, they are constantly alert to the modes that patients bring to the sessions, and to the possibility that modes are triggered in response to events in the relationship itself. This requires a continuous ability to reflect on the "here-and-now," and to use instances that emerge as opportunities for emotional learning.

Schema therapists do not shy away from triggering patients' schemas if necessary (though they will not intentionally do this only for the sake of activating schemas). Still, schemas invariably get triggered, whether in therapy or out of it, and whether the therapist is particularly cautious or not. Instead of preventing the activation of a schema, the schema therapist focuses on processing this activation and trying to maximize the psychological growth that can emerge from it.

A common instance of schema triggering appears in what Safran and Muran (1996) call "therapeutic ruptures." In such ruptures, the bond between the patient and the therapist deteriorates, sometimes very rapidly. For example, the therapist may inadvertently make a comment that leads a patient with an Emotional Deprivation schema to feel misunderstood or judged. (As an aside, a similar comment may very well lead a patient with a different schema to react with different thoughts and feelings – a Subjugation schema may lead to feeling controlled, an Entitlement schema to feeling slighted, and so on.) Often, these feelings lead the patient to react: usually, with withdrawal, but at times with expressions of anger or displeasure.

Rather than minimizing what has happened ("Oh, you misunderstood, I meant something completely different"), the schema therapist seizes the opportunity. First, the therapist notes and acknowledges the rupture. This could be done by saying, "I notice you became very quiet in the last minute" or "Wait, let's see what just happened between us." Framing it as something that is happening in the here-and-now, and within the relationship, is consistent with the view that interpersonal ruptures are not "my fault" or "your fault" – instead, they are relational events.

If patients are able to acknowledge their anger or disappointment, therapists empathize and take responsibility for their contribution to the rupture. At times, the therapist can do this even without the patient's acknowledgement; indeed, seeing the therapist apologize, take responsibility, and empathize with the patient's hurt or anger may model for some patients the possibility of both feeling and expressing negative emotions safely within a caring relationship.

When a patient continues to withdraw and does not acknowledge his or her feelings, the therapist may focus on the withdrawal itself: "You say that you're not angry at me, but it makes me wonder why not. Putting myself in your shoes, I can easily imagine getting pretty upset. What do you think will happen if you did get angry at me?" By exploring this question, the therapist is inviting the Healthy Adult mode in the patient to become engaged. It often takes multiple invitations of this sort, across different situations, before an avoidant or withdrawing patient begins to tentatively accept it.

A second step in handling any rupture such as this involves linking the particular instance to underlying schemas, modes, or coping styles. Once both therapist and patient are focused on the here-and-now, and have some sense of the thoughts, feelings, and behavioral impulses that have emerged, it is possible to create the historical link: "Do you remember having a similar feeling with other people in your life?" Sometimes, the link may already be evident to the therapist or the patient, and can be stated explicitly: "You know, I wonder if my comment, or maybe the tone of voice I had, reminded you of the way your parents used to respond when you had a problem; I just pushed those same buttons they used to push, that made you feel so misunderstood and judged [or subjugated, etc.]?"

One outcome of this exploration is the understanding that a particular schema was triggered, and that there is some similarity between the current event and other events in the past. The therapist may then suggest to the patient to address the recognized schema (e.g., using cognitive techniques; see Point 21). But the strength of attending to here-and-now events comes from their immediacy and poignancy. To capitalize on them, it is often useful to go beyond cognitive techniques. The therapist may choose this moment to engage in some role-playing or other behavioral or experiential techniques (see Points 22 and 23). Introducing behavioral techniques can strengthen the patient's capacity to act differently when similar triggers or ruptures occur in the future, either in therapy or in other relationships. And incorporating experiential techniques can deepen the emotional understanding of the linkage between the particular event, its trigger, and the schemas that underlie it.

21

# Toolbox 2: Cognitive techniques

Once the patient and therapist have established a case formulation, they have also identified a set of cognitive change goals: namely, the weakening of the existing maladaptive schemas and the strengthening of an alternative, healthy set of schemas. The same change goals can be phrased in mode terms too: cognitive techniques strengthen the way of thinking associated with the Healthy Adult mode, and weaken the ways of thinking that characterize maladaptive coping and parent modes.

A wide range of cognitive techniques are available to the schema therapist. Many of these are similar to methods used in other forms of CBT; schema therapists are encouraged to borrow freely from these and to develop (or improvise with) additional cognitive tools when appropriate. The most widely used cognitive tools are as follows.

## *Collecting data/evidence*

Early in the therapy, many schema therapists introduce the use of schema diaries or of other self-monitoring logs such as daily records of thoughts/feelings/behaviors. We devote a special section to schema diaries (and the related schema flashcards); here, we discuss the schema therapist's use of the rudimentary monitoring sheets often used in other forms of CBT. (For an example of a monitoring record sheet, see Figure 21.1.)

When first introduced, these monitoring sheets are completed in-session with the therapist's aid. Later, they are assigned as homework. We already discussed the use of these records in the assessment phase (see Point 16). In the schema change phase, these records first provide a tangible way of developing some

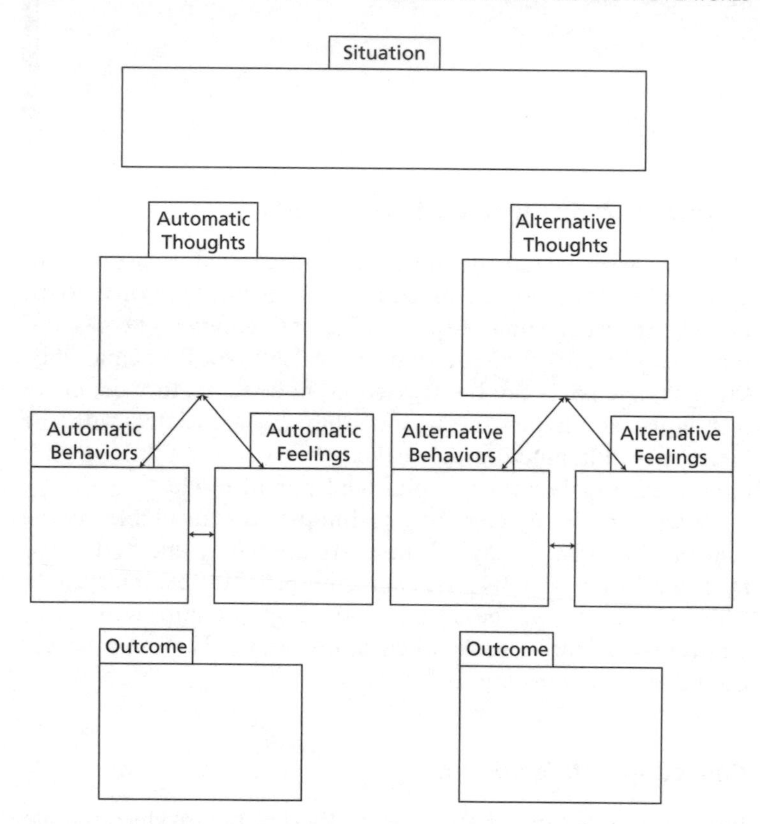


**Figure 21.1** Daily thought record form

reflective distance from upsetting events. Initially, the patient is asked to record one particular event each day, and to note only their automatic thoughts, feelings, and behaviors in response to this event. Later on, the patient can be taught ways of questioning the automatic thoughts, identifying the schemas that drive them, and providing alternative, healthier responses to the same activating events. Yet even the initial use of the daily record (i.e., prior to developing any alternative response, or "disputation" as it is referred to in Rational Emotive Behavior

Therapy) puts a wedge between the (objective) activating event and the (subjective and schema-driven) response to it. Once this wedge is in, the patient can be taught to test the evidence for and against their schema-driven view, and to rationally determine whether this view is accurate or, as is often the case, biased.

A related cognitive technique, first developed by Padesky (1994), is the Positive Data Log. Unlike daily records (which tend to be completed in reaction to upsetting events, typically ones that trigger the maladaptive schemas first), patients completing this Log are asked to actively monitor their day-to-day life for events and evidence that is consistent with the healthy and adaptive alternative schemas. This is usually a very difficult task at first but, if done slowly and with much encouragement, can be quite powerful. To do so, the therapist should first introduce the Log (and add to it) within the session and not as homework. The rationale for the Log should be presented clearly and reviewed periodically, and the (almost inevitable) difficulties that arise in completing the Log should be discussed (and processed, possibly by using a daily record or a schema diary, discussed below).

A third method of carefully collecting and examining the evidence for and against a schema is the Historical Life Review. In this Review, the patient and therapist generate confirming and disconfirming evidence for the schema at different points of the patient's lifetime (e.g., infancy, toddlerhood, childhood, early adolescence, etc.). Once the evidence for and against the schema (e.g., "I'm incompetent" or "I'm unlovable") is fleshed out, the patient and the therapist review it and summarize what the evidence suggests. In most cases, doing so will clarify the lack of evidence for the veracity of the schema view and the origins of its development.

### *Reframing/reattribution*

Reframing involves providing a different cognitive frame (or explanation) than the one automatically generated for an event, problem, or situation. For example, a patient who experiences a setback and who automatically judges himself to be "incompetent, a loser, a failure" can gain from reframing the situation. A typical reframe in CBT reattributes the setback from the person himself to his actions or his skill ("you didn't do well this time, but that doesn't mean you are a failure"; "you haven't mastered this one particular skill, and it was really needed in this instance. Let's see if we can think of a way for you to master it"). Such reframing occurs in Schema Therapy as well, and in addition, Schema Therapy uses reattribution to help create a healthier view of schemas and their origins. For example, the therapist may help the patient reattribute his current life problem to a schema (e.g., Defectiveness/Shame), a maladaptive coping response (Surrender), or a mode (Critical Parent), rather than seeing it as inherent to the patient himself.

### *Schema flashcards and diaries*

Schema flashcards provide very structured guidance for reattributing difficult (and recurring) situations in daily life. Flashcards are written summaries of the healthy response to a schema trigger, designed to be carried around by the patient and used on-the-spot, in moments when schemas get triggered. Flashcards are completed jointly in the session and require the collection of sufficient data as well as the development of a clear (and well understood) reframing for the schema. The flashcard then notes the most powerful evidence against the schema view, along with the most powerful healthy responses to this view. Flashcards have a set template, into which the therapist and the patient put phrases that are relevant to the patient's experience. A completed flashcard may read as follows (*italics* denote the sections completed by the patient and therapist):

> Right now I'm feeling *depressed about my inability to do my job* because *I just failed to complete another assignment at*

*work, and I anticipate that my boss will be impatient or even harsh with me*. However, I know that these are probably my *Defectiveness, Failure, and Unrelenting Standards schemas* being triggered. I learned these through *my mother's repeated criticism and perfectionistic attitude toward herself and me*. These schemas lead me to exaggerate the degree to which *setbacks, even if real, will be disastrous*.

Even though I believe *that my incompetence will be found out and I will lose my job or be humiliated*, the reality is that *I actually have a pretty good record at work, and my boss knows this (and usually reminds me of it herself). Even if I don't complete this task on time, I won't fall that far behind schedule*. The evidence in my life supporting this healthy view includes: *the fact that my performance reviews have consistently been good even when I felt very anxious in anticipation of them; the praise I got from my boss about the last project, and the fact that she turns to me for advice on how to do certain things, even as recently as last week*. Therefore, even though I feel like *there's no point even trying, because I'll never finish this task – and I feel like just shutting down and not asking for help*, I could instead *give her a call, talk through the parts that I'm struggling with, and figure out a new timeline that will allow me to finish this task without feeling like I'm losing my mind*.

Flashcards can be created for most types of events, particularly ones that are likely to recur. In addition, schema diaries offer a more advanced and flexible tool that can be used as needed by the patient when schemas are triggered in novel or different situations. The diary begins, like a daily monitoring record, with rubrics for identifying the trigger (activating event), emotions, thoughts, and behaviors. It then requires the patient to identify the schemas that were triggered and to note similar childhood and adolescent experiences (i.e., developmental precursors to the current schema triggers). The patient is asked to note which of their reactions were realistic and which were not (e.g., did they do anything to worsen the situation? Did they misinterpret or exaggerate the situation?). They are then asked to note a healthy view of the situation (essentially, a cognitive reframing) and to note healthy behaviors (essentially, ways of problem-focused or emotion-focused coping).

### *Schema dialogues*

Dialogue techniques assume that the patient has already learned to identify the existence of both a schema side and a healthy side. The therapist may then invite the patient to engage in dialogue or role-plays involving these sides. Patients sometimes feel uncomfortable using these techniques; though the decision to engage in them should ultimately be a collaborative one, patients often respond to the therapist's gentle encouragement to experiment with the technique.

When first engaging in a schema dialogue, the patient plays the schema side, and the therapist plays the healthy side. The therapist might invite the patient to use the technique in this manner: "Let's have a debate between the schema side and the healthy side. You play the schema side, and I'll play the healthy side. Your job is to try as hard as you can to prove that the schema is correct, and mine is to try as hard as I can to prove that the schema is wrong." We begin in this manner because initially, patients have very little experience voicing their healthy side and can benefit from observing the therapist do so. Additionally, having patients begin by expressing the schema side helps obtain a richer and more fleshed-out understanding of the thoughts and feelings enclosed in the schema view, and allows the therapist to come up with counterpoints to whatever arguments are raised by the schema side.

Eventually, the patient takes on the healthy side, and is asked to counter the schema's arguments and to come up with healthy responses. This is often difficult and requires coaching, or modeling, on the therapist's side. Thus, depending on the ease with which the patient moves into the healthy side, the therapist may play the schema side, or may act as a coach, with the patient alternating between the healthy and the schema sides. In the first scenario (the therapist playing the schema side), it is often useful for the patient and therapist to switch chairs. In the second (the therapist as coach), the patient may alternate between two different chairs, with the therapist standing "on the sidelines" of the debate, as would a coach (see Point 22 for a lengthier description of experiential techniques, including chair-work; also see Kellogg, 2004).

In either case, it is imperative that the dialogue proceeds until the healthy side prevails. The patient alone may not be able to reach this outcome at first. It is the therapist's role to offer just enough encouragement to ensure that the healthy side has the final word every time. As this exercise is repeated (a repetition which is essential in most cases), the therapist is likely to move further and further back, while the patient reaches the ability to conduct the dialogue independently.

22

# Toolbox 3: Emotion-focused techniques

Emotion-focused techniques are some of the most powerful tools at the schema therapist's disposal for healing early maladaptive schemas. The therapist often begins the change phase of Schema Therapy by using cognitive techniques such as thought records, schema flashcards, and schema diaries to alter early maladaptive schemas. These methods help the patient to achieve some intellectual distance from the schemas. However, the intense emotions attached to the schemas usually still remain. The patient says, "Now I see that I'm not defective; rather, I have a Defectiveness schema. However, I still *feel* defective." The purpose of emotion-focused techniques is to help the patient feel different, that is, to take away the schemas' emotional power.

The most important emotion-focused techniques in Schema Therapy are role-playing and guided imagery, although Schema Therapy also makes use of other emotional methods such as letter writing (Young et al., 2003). Schema Therapy borrows role-playing techniques from Gestalt Therapy (Kellogg, 2004). Role-playing is a flexible method in which the therapist asks the patient to play various roles, such as different sides of himself, his parents, or other significant figures from his life, either from the past or the present. The therapist asks the patient to switch back and forth between roles, so that the patient carries out dialogues between them. The therapist may also play roles, taking part in the dialogues himself.

The two-chair method is the best known of these techniques. The patient sits in one chair when he plays one role, then switches chairs when assuming a different role. More than two chairs may be used to accommodate multiple roles. When switching chairs, patients "embody" the roles they are playing, making the feelings, thoughts, memories, and physical sensations associated with each role more alive and palpable (Kellogg, 2004). The therapists stage-manage the "action" in the scenes that are being created, assume the role of actor when they step into the scenes themselves, and reassume the role of therapist, coaching the patient when necessary, observing the patient's reactions, and commenting on the action taking place.

Imagery techniques share much in common with role-play methods. However, they can be an even more powerful means of accessing the patient's Vulnerable Child mode, enabling the therapist to heal the patient's early wounds (i.e., schemas) directly. As noted earlier, patients routinely use avoidance as a strategy to escape from emotional pain. When therapists ask the patient to close their eyes and allow a scene from childhood to emerge spontaneously, they bypass the patients' coping modes. The images that emerge are nearly always connected to painful events in which the patients' early developmental needs went unmet, giving rise to early maladaptive schemas.

These experiential techniques share common mechanisms. Cognitive therapy has, until recently, tended to emphasize the idea that maladaptive schemas involve distorted ways of thinking; in contrast, it has paid less attention to the affective components of schemas. However, research now demonstrates that schemas are easiest to change when cognitions are "hot," that is, when they are activated along with the emotions that are associated with them (David & Szentagotai, 2006). The emotion-focused techniques capitalize on this principle by triggering schemas, so that the cognitions, emotions, bodily sensations, and memories associated with them become active.

Moreover, the experiences that give rise to schemas are often non-verbal in nature. For example, a child who sits alone in his room waiting for his parent to return home, or witnesses a fight between his parents, or is subjected to physical, emotional, or sexual abuse, has an experience that is largely emotional and non-verbal in nature. Many of the experiences that give rise to schemas may even predate the development of language, and are therefore inherently preverbal. Of course, the child is likely to be able to reflect verbally about these experiences (e.g., "Nobody wants to be with me," "It is my fault that my parents are fighting"). However, much of what he experiences will be encoded non-verbally: as visual images, bodily sensations, or emotions (Smucker & Boos, 2005). These considerations suggest that emotion-focused techniques may be the most effective means of altering the non-verbal, affective components of schemas.

Emotion-focused techniques serve a further purpose. Avoidance is a primary mechanism through which people cope with painful affects (Borkovec et al., 2004). When patients talk about experiences in an overly rational, detached manner that avoids real emotions, their schemas are likely to remain unchanged. Emotion-focused techniques bypass these avoidant forms of coping. They access affective memories directly, enabling them to be reprocessed more effectively.

23

# Toolbox 4: Behavioral pattern-breaking

The final toolbox in Schema Therapy involves behavioral pattern-breaking techniques, focused on behavioral change. The application of these techniques leads to a replacement of existing, schema-driven patterns of action with healthier, adaptive behaviors. The goal, therefore, is to generalize insights and knowledge acquired in Schema Therapy – because these, alone, do not automatically translate into acting differently or more adaptively.

Behavioral pattern-breaking usually takes the longest time and continues into later stages of therapy, after earlier (relational, cognitive, and affective) changes have already taken place. Nonetheless, since Schema Therapy is often implemented after a course of CBT for Axis I problems, certain behavioral techniques (e.g., exposure, response prevention, rehearsal, activity scheduling, behavioral experimentation) may already be familiar to the patient and may be used at an earlier point.

The specific targets for behavioral change are those schema-driven coping behaviors that, left untouched, serve to perpetuate the schemas. For example, for someone with an Abandonment schema, maladaptive behaviors may include selecting unavailable and distant partners (surrender coping style), clinging or pushing partners away pre-emptively (overcompensation coping style), or avoiding intimacy altogether (avoidant coping style).

A good way to guide the behavioral work to the most important targets for change is to review (and possibly revise) the case conceptualization that was created in the assessment phase, with an eye particularly on the sections devoted to coping behaviors. Once particular behaviors are chosen as targets, the therapist and the patient work on describing them in as much detail as possible. What triggers the behaviors? What happens as the behavior unfolds? What are the usual consequences of the behavior? When patients struggle to answer these questions, the therapist may suggest using imagery to vividly recall a triggering situation and to help fill in details about the pattern itself, and about thoughts and feelings that accompany it.

Some of the common techniques that may be used are as follows.

### *Developing a schema flashcard focused on alternative healthy behaviors*

For example, a patient who often uses the surrender coping style to manage a painful Abandonment schema may develop a schema flashcard reviewing her typical responses (e.g., seeking out relationships with married or involved men) and their schema origins; the flashcard would then include instructions for behaving differently (e.g., seeking out higher-potential relationships; soothing oneself when feeling alone).

### *Rehearsing a behavior in imagery or role-play*

To increase the likelihood that a new behavior will be carried out, patients would be encouraged to role-play it in the session, as well as to close their eyes and vividly imagine a relevant situation where the behavior may be possible. For example, the patient described above may need to rehearse approaching a potential date or politely declining advances from inappropriate partners.

### *Assigning behavioral homework*

As we know from cognitive behavioral therapy, successful behavioral planning often benefits from taking a difficult behavior, breaking it down, and then making a personal (and public) commitment to engage in the behavior. For example, the patient described above could recruit the therapist's help in tackling a large task (e.g., re-entering the dating world). Particular steps towards this large goal (e.g., signing up to a dating site) could be assigned as homework, and progress towards the behavior could then be reviewed in the next session. This approach increases the likelihood that patients would feel accountable to themselves, and also provides a chance for the therapist to reinforce healthy behavior.

### *Associating behaviors with self-administered rewards and contingencies*

The therapist and the patient can discuss the option of using positive contingencies as rewards for healthy behaviors. The specific rewards would differ from one person to another (buying oneself a small gift, giving oneself permission to do something self-nurturing, calling the therapist and leaving a message announcing the successful completion of the homework assignment).

In extreme cases, when the patient is consistently unable to achieve behavioral change, the therapist may suggest a break from therapy as a contingent response to the lack of healthy behavior. The therapist would present this as an issue of readiness for change – and would commit to resuming therapy as soon as the patient is ready. Note that this is a rare suggestion, made only when the therapist believes that other benefits of remaining in therapy do not outweigh the lack of progress toward the behavioral change goal. When it is used, it is often best to suggest "one last try" – a period of concerted effort before taking the break from therapy: "How would you feel about continuing for three to four more weeks to see if you're able to make these changes we've discussed; if not, we could discontinue meeting for a while, and you can call me when you feel ready to resume treatment?"

24

## Mode dialogues and imagery

Mode work builds on the various tools we have presented, but particularly on the emotion-focused techniques of dialogues and imagery.

### *Dialogues in mode work*

The "schema dialogue" is the simplest form of role-play used by schema therapists. Therapists ask patients to play the side of their schemas and then switch chairs to assume the role of the Healthy Adult. The Healthy Adult challenges the patient's schema side, using arguments and evidence that counter the schema side's distorted views. This method shares much in common with the cognitive therapy technique known as "collaborative empiricism," in which patient and therapist work together to test the validity of the patient's beliefs (Segal & Shaw, 1996). However, because it is also an experiential technique, the schema dialogue has the advantage of activating the patient's schemas, which, as noted above, enhances its effectiveness.

Role-playing is especially effective when combined with schema mode work. In mode work, therapists ask patients to play different sides of themselves (i.e., different modes), switching chairs as they assume the role of different modes. For example, the therapist may ask the patient to switch back and forth between the Detached Protector side, which fears and avoids emotions, and the Vulnerable Child, which needs emotional contact. Or the therapist may ask another patient to play the role of the Angry Child, and vent her pent-up anger at the Punitive Parent.

Because these dialogues don't follow a predetermined script, there is room for unexpected developments that can enrich the exercise. For example, we often witness the spontaneous emergence of additional modes that shed light on the patient's difficulties. The therapist can also introduce new characters (e.g., a healthier mode, or a supportive adult caregiver), or can "rescript" past painful or traumatic scenes, enabling the patient to experience new, corrective emotional experiences to take the place of old ones. For example, the therapist can help the Vulnerable Child express his needs directly to the Punitive Parent, rather than keeping them to himself (Smucker & Boos, 2005; Young et al., 2003).

### *Imagery in mode work*

Imagery is used in Schema Therapy for assessment purposes (see Point 17) and to promote schema change. When used for schema change, imagery involves rescripting, where the therapist alters elements from the painful or traumatic scenes that the patient experienced to help promote schema healing via reparenting (Young et al., 2003). Therapists usually begin by asking patients to close their eyes and imagine a scene from the present that is currently bothering them. By focusing on a current, upsetting scene, the therapist works with the schemas that are currently active. The therapist asks the patient to vividly describe the scene in the present tense, as if it is currently taking place, providing details about what they and the other people in the scene are doing, feeling, and thinking. As the patient describes the scene in rich detail, the emotions associated with it increase in intensity. The therapist then asks the patient to let go of the image, but hold onto the feeling associated with it, and "travel back" to the past, to childhood, and allow another image to emerge that has the same or a similar feeling to the one that was just experienced. This new image from the patient's childhood almost always shares schemas with the one from the present situation, enabling the patient to understand the way in which these themes from the past play themselves out in present life.

As patients relive the scene from the past, they are able to vent their feelings of grief, fear, shame, guilt, or rage from these painful events. The therapist mostly listens, facilitating the process by asking the patient to provide further details. As this process takes place, the therapist evaluates the child's unmet or frustrated developmental needs, and the schemas and coping responses (or modes) that arose from them. The therapist then asks the patient's permission to enter the image to provide for some of what the child needed, but wasn't able to get at the time the events occurred. By entering the image himself, the therapist is able to reparent the child directly, providing, for example, comfort, validation, or protection, depending on the child's needs. These experiences of reparenting via imagery are among the most powerful at the schema therapist's disposal for healing the patient's early wounds. Patients often describe these imagery exercises as some of their most beneficial experiences in Schema Therapy.

Schema Therapy's use of imagery and rescripting takes a somewhat different form when the patient's early experiences are traumatic ones. First, the therapist usually waits until later in the therapy to conduct such imagery, until the patient is strong enough to sustain it without a risk of decompensation or retraumatization. Second, the therapist introduces techniques to help the patient to feel safer and more "in control" of the imagery experience, for example, beginning and ending the imagery with a "safe place" image, and limiting the amount of time spent in the image. Finally, the therapist intervenes quickly and forcefully when the image is a traumatic one. The therapist interrupts the scene as soon as it becomes traumatic, and asks the patient for permission to enter the image to protect the child. Therapists then take whatever steps are necessary to protect the child in the image, for example, by placing themselves between an abusive parent and the child and preventing the parent from committing the abuse.

The effectiveness of various imagery techniques in working through traumatic experiences has been supported by considerable research (Davidson & Parker, 2001; Foa et al., 2005; Smucker & Boos, 2005). However, the form of rescripting used by schema therapists is distinguished from other forms in certain important respects. For example, compared with prolonged exposure methods (Foa, Hembree, & Rothbaum 2007), long a staple of behavior therapists, schema therapists spend less time having patients relive traumatic experiences, and instead intervene quickly to protect the child in the image. Compared with EMDR (Davidson & Parker, 2001), another trauma reprocessing method, schema therapists are more guided in their approach, rescripting traumatic memories to help meet the patient's early developmental needs, rather than following the patient's free associations stemming from the trauma. Thus, while sharing certain elements in common with other imagery methods, Schema Therapy places more emphasis on providing a corrective emotional experience to heal the patient's early traumas.

# 25

## Specific points for working with borderline personality disorder

Schema Therapy has gained the greatest amount of recognition and research support as an approach for the treatment of borderline personality disorder (BPD). Individuals with this disorder suffer from wide-ranging volatility. This volatility or instability occurs in their emotions, interpersonal relationships, self-view, and in their ability to regulate their own behaviors. It leads to intense rage, startling impulsivity, and a life marked by frequent crises, including suicidal or self-injurious acts. These individuals are in recurrent and severe emotional pain, and pain often becomes a part of life for their loved ones as well.

BPD is thought to emerge from an interaction of temperamental vulnerabilities and traumatic (or at the very least invalidating) environments in early development. The biological factors underlying BPD seem to be a labile and emotional temperament, which manifests itself in infancy and childhood as difficulty being soothed. It tends to contribute to, or at least go hand-in-hand with, insecure attachment bonds. However, these could very well be the result of environmental/familial factors. Schema Therapy (e.g., Young et al., 2003) identifies four such factors that are common in the early experiences of adults who go on to develop BPD: instability and lack of safety; emotional deprivation; punitive and rejecting parental practices; and/or subjugating home environments, in which the needs of the children are seen as secondary to those of their parents.

For years, the diagnosis of BPD in a patient was seen as a warning sign to clinicians – "beware, difficult or even untreatable patient." However, the past two decades have brought encouraging news about greater understanding of the disorder itself, along with effective treatments for it. It has been conceptualized as a disorder of emotion dysregulation (Linehan, 1993), of negative and dysfunctional core beliefs (Butler, Brown, Beck, & Grisham, 2002), of poorly developed object relations (Kernberg, 1976), and of disorganized attachment bonds leading to an inability to mentalize (Bateman & Fonagy, 2004). Each of these approaches has led to treatment models that are promising in their results.

Importantly, these conceptualizations need not be mutually exclusive. Instead, this complex disorder with its manifold cognitive, affective, behavioral, and interpersonal symptoms almost cries out for an integrative treatment approach, one that addresses both present symptoms and past development. Schema Therapy offers such an integrative approach, and explicitly uses cognitive, affective, behavioral, and interpersonal tools (see Points 20–23). The notion of schema modes (see Points 8–13) was introduced into Schema Therapy precisely to help understand and treat the cardinal symptom of BPD: namely, instability.

### *Applying the Schema Therapy model to BPD*

Though patients with BPD evidence many (or even most) of the early maladaptive schemas, the notion of chronic, pervasive schemas leaves the key symptom of instability unexplained. This was the main impetus for the development of the mode concept. Modes are temporary and fluctuating states that include distinct moods, motivations, memories, images, and thoughts. As clinicians familiar with the disorder know, individuals with BPD often alternate quite abruptly and with great intensity, between extreme emotional and motivational states: of anger or self-loathing, of idealization or devaluation, of intense feeling and numb emptiness. In Schema Therapy, we see these fluctuations as shifts among a relatively fixed set of schema modes, described next.

The schema modes most prominently seen in BPD are the Detached Protector (a unique form of the avoidant maladaptive coping mode); the Abandoned/Abused Child (again, a unique form of the Vulnerable Child mode); the Angry/Impulsive Child mode, the Punitive Parent mode, and the Healthy Adult mode (often quite weakened or even entirely silent).

The vulnerability of patients with BPD resides within their Abandoned/Abused Child mode. This mode contains the memories, feelings, sensations, and thoughts of the patient as a young child, at the time (or times) when the abuse, invalidation, maltreatment, or abandonment were most pronounced. When in the Abandoned/Abused Child mode, patients are very threatened, needy, almost inconsolable, and may speak and act as little children. To help our adult patients grasp this mode, and to help them empathize as much as possible with this hurt child within themselves, we often refer to this mode as "Little [patient's name]"; for example, for a patient named Caroline, this mode would be referred to as Little Caroline.

Open, unabashed vulnerability is often unexpressed in BPD. Instead, when present-day events (in or out of therapy) trigger patients' schemas, they very frequently "flip" into the Angry/Impulsive Child mode. For example, when Caroline is offended by a relationship partner, she has great difficulty expressing her distress and vulnerability directly. In its place, Caroline may become frustrated or furious – a mode we may refer to as "Angry Caroline." This mode has its roots in the early attempts to fight back against unfair, invalidating treatment. Often, it was through these angry or impulsive outbursts that the patient (as a child) got at least some reprieve from the distress, victimization, or invalidation that was common in early life. The logic governing this mode is of course faulty: rather than leading to long-term gains, the impulsive or aggressive acts of this mode can make bad situations worse. But cool logic is not the strong suit of this mode.

At times, the angry or impulsive outbursts activate the patient's Punitive Parent mode: the internalized voice of the harsh, punitive, invalidating figure – usually a parent – whose behavior towards the patient as a child is most clearly seen as the source of the hurt and vulnerability. When in this mode, patients often assume a dismissive tone towards themselves (and sometimes towards others, including the therapist). Rather than showing compassion or empathy for their own difficulties, they are contemptuous, impatient, and self-blaming. Importantly, this mode (just like the people after whom it is modeled) does not reserve its punitiveness for the patient's angry or impulsive outbursts. Instead, almost any behavior – but particularly displays of child-like vulnerability – would bring about harsh treatment. And once there, the mode makes it much harder to access, or maintain any contact with, the patients' vulnerable side.

Finally, and in contrast to the widely-held picture of BPD patients as constantly emotional, we have found the most prevalent mode in patients' daily life to be the Detached Protector mode. When in this mode, patients appear externally to be calm and in control, while internally they are attempting to numb out all feelings and emotional needs. The Detached Protector, as its name implies, tries to shield and distance the person from the feelings of fear, vulnerability, rejection, and defectiveness (the Abandoned/Abused Child mode), to avoid the self-critical and harsh voice (Punitive Parent mode), and to keep the rage and the behavioral outbursts (of the Angry/Impulsive Child mode) at bay. The rule that governs the Detached Protector is "it is better not to feel anything." To follow this rule, it uses all sorts of cognitive or behavioral avoidance strategies, including social distancing (i.e., pushing people away), mental dissociation, substance abuse, and self-injury (as an attempt to mask emotional pain with physical pain).

### *Treating BPD with Schema Therapy*

The general goal in treating patients with BPD is to help strengthen the mostly absent Healthy Adult mode, so that it, in turn, can nurture the Abandoned/Abused Child, empathize with – but place limits on – the Angry/Impulsive Child, and fight tooth-and-nail against the Punitive Parent voice. Before any of these can happen, the patient must be cajoled into allowing the Detached Protector mode to step aside and allow the therapist (and later, the patient's own Healthy Adult mode) to gain access. This is quite difficult – the strategies of the Detached Protector are often seen by patients as the one thing that has kept them safe or has allowed them to survive. The obstacle posed by the Detached Protector, and the complexity of the therapy as a whole, dictate both greater length and greater intensity for therapy with BPD: typically, patients are seen twice weekly and the therapy usually requires 2–3 years or more (though gains begin to be seen within the first year).

Schema Therapy with patients who have BPD progresses through three major stages. In the first stage, the therapist builds a reparenting bond of trust and rapport, bypasses the Detached Protector, and becomes a source of nurturance for the patient. In the second phase, the objective is to create change in the schema modes: to continue replacing the Detached Protector with the Healthy Adult, to expunge the Punitive Parent, to set limits on the Angry/Impulsive Child, and to nurture and empower the Abandoned/Abused Child. This stage is, in a sense, the heart of the therapy. It is followed by a third and final stage of autonomy building, in which therapy gains are generalized, particularly through practical behavioral steps, as well as through a gradual "weaning" off the therapy.

These stages and goals are pursued from the same stances and with the same methods described throughout this book – only more so. Patients with BPD often have previous unsatisfying experiences with therapy. By definition, they are wary of trusting any caregiver. And they are, objectively, more demanding (i.e., more needy) than the average patient. Thus, there are unique challenges to conducting Schema Therapy with these patients:

(a) **Suicidal or self-injurious behavior**: Patients with BPD are very often impulsive and self-injurious; less frequently (but still, in alarming rates) they also attempt or even complete suicide. When these behaviors emerge, the schema therapist responds by: (1) increasing contact with the patient and assessing suicidality at each contact; (2) obtaining permission to contact and involve significant others; and (3) discussing or arranging for adjunctive treatments (medication, hospitalization, or consultation with a peer).

(b) **Therapy-interfering behaviors, or ones that impinge on the therapist's rights**: In this category are such behaviors as absences and breaks in therapy, failing to respect the therapist's boundaries, and failing to follow through on key therapy agreements (e.g., the commitment to contact the therapist before, not after, they act on a suicidal urge). In these cases, schema therapists follow these guidelines: (1) First, the limits are reviewed with the patient in a personal way (e.g., "I am concerned about you and therefore need you to do this") rather than impersonal one (e.g., "We have a policy regarding absences in our clinic"). (2) These limits need to be set at the first instance of a behavior, so that they do not seem arbitrary or punitive. (3) The therapist sets natural consequences for violating the limits (e.g., restraining the number or length of phone calls that the therapist would take between sessions). (4) If the problematic behavior recurs, the therapist expresses firm disapproval and carries out the promised consequence, and sets further consequences for any future problematic behavior. These should be progressively more serious and, depending on the severity of the behavior, may ultimately entail a temporary break in therapy or even a permanent termination of the therapy.

(c) **Angry behavior towards the therapist**: In two of the characteristic modes (Angry/Impulsive Child and Punitive Parent) we come to expect the patient with BPD to have angry outbursts. The therapist's first task is to determine whether the concern underlying the outburst is valid – and if so, to validate it. In most cases, the therapist will follow these steps: (1) allowing the patient to ventilate their anger fully; (2) empathizing with the unmet need that underlies the anger; (3) engaging the patient in reality testing; and (4) rehearsing appropriate assertiveness.

(d) **Mistaking the Detached Protector for a Healthy Adult**: A common problem in the treatment of higher-functioning patients is that of misperceiving seemingly rational words or actions on the part of the patient to reflect the actions of a Healthy Adult mode, rather than a Detached Protector mode. The way to distinguish the two, of course, is to determine whether the patient is experiencing any affect; if not, it is more likely the Detached Protector that is present.

(e) **Assessment/conceptualization**: Since patients with BPD will endorse most, or even all, of the items on the Young Schema Questionnaire, we often refrain from using this instrument (as well as other self-report inventories) early in the therapy. The incremental information obtained from them is minimal, whereas the experience of endorsing item after negative item on them can be very upsetting for the patient. Moreover, the therapy with such patients will focus more on modes, and less on schemas per se.

(f) **Introducing experiential work (e.g., imagery) too early**: The use of experiential techniques for processing traumatic memories is an essential part of Schema Therapy for BPD. However, because of the heightened vulnerability of the Abandoned/Abused Child, the preparation for imagery or other experiential interventions should be done with extra caution. Before setting out to conduct these, we strongly recommend reviewing the relevant chapters in Young et al. (2003). We also recommend a short book (Arntz & van Genderen, 2009) devoted explicitly to Schema Therapy for BPD.

## *Research support for Schema Therapy in BPD*

Since 2005, three studies have examined the efficacy of Schema Therapy in BPD. The largest of these, a randomized control trial (Giesen-Bloo et al., 2006) compared the efficacy of Schema Therapy with that of another established treatment for BPD: transference focused psychotherapy (TFP), developed by Kernberg and his colleagues (Clarkin, Yeomans, & Kernberg, 1999). Eighty-eight patients with BPD were randomly assigned to one of the two treatments, both comprising two weekly 50-minute outpatient sessions for 3 years. Analyses were conducted at both 1 and 3 years. Both groups improved on personality constructs, but Schema Therapy was superior on all outcome measures, including recovery (45.5% in Schema Therapy, 23.8% in TFP) and/or reliable change in BPD symptoms rated by independent interviewers (65.9% and 42.9%, respectively). Similar results were found with self-reported quality of life and psychopathology. Importantly (given the topic of patient retention discussed earlier), the dropout rates were considerably higher for TFP (50%) than for Schema Therapy (25%). Among those who dropped out, Schema Therapy patients had a median of 98 sessions (close to 1 year) vs. 34 sessions (roughly 4 months) for TFP patients.

A second study (Farrell, Shaw, & Webber, 2009) randomized 32 severely symptomatic patients to individual treatment as usual (TAU) or to TAU augmented by 8 months of weekly group Schema Therapy. The Schema Therapy group focused primarily on creating a strong therapeutic alliance, fostering validation, emotional awareness, distress tolerance, and schema change. The study found considerable reductions in self-reported and clinician-rated borderline symptoms ($d = 2.48$ and 4.29, respectively), as well as in general symptomatology and global functioning ($d = .72$ and 1.80, respectively). The corresponding effect sizes in the TAU group were not significant (.09, .49, –.25, and .14). Importantly, a 6-month follow-up revealed that the effects only strengthened with time for the

Schema Therapy group, but not for the control group. For example, 0% of the Schema Therapy group, but 83% of the control group, met criteria for BPD at follow-up.

A third study (Nordahl & Nysaeter, 2005) demonstrated the efficacy of Schema Therapy using a single-case series design. Six women with BPD were assessed at baseline on three occasions over 10 weeks, and showed no symptomatic reduction. They then began individual Schema Therapy, with weekly sessions over 18–36 months. They were assessed after 20 and 40 sessions, at termination, and at a 12–16-month follow-up. By follow-up, three of the six no longer met criteria for BPD, and all exhibited a reduction in symptoms (d = 1.8). None had attempted suicide and all but one showed a reduction in other self-injurious behaviors.

# 26

# Specific points for working with narcissistic personality disorder and antisocial personality disorder

## *Treating narcissistic personality disorder with Schema Therapy*

As noted earlier (see Point 7), narcissistic personality disorder (NPD) is perhaps the quintessential example of a personality disorder based on an overcompensating coping style. The patient "turns the tables" on other people by adopting a superior, arrogant, devaluing stance, which serves to compensate for underlying schemas such as Defectiveness and Emotional Deprivation. Many authors have theorized that NPD develops as a result of the parent's egoistic use of the child (Ronningstam, 2009). The parent overvalues the child's "special" qualities such as beauty, talent, or intelligence, which affirm the parent's own sense of specialness, while ignoring the child's basic emotional needs such as warmth, nurturance, and acceptance. As a result, the child's identity coalesces around a grandiose self-image, which masks underlying feelings of emptiness, loneliness, or inferiority.

In schema mode terms, the child learns to overcompensate for his schemas by developing a Self-aggrandizer mode, a side that feels superior, "super-special," and powerful. However, there remains, usually hidden from view, another side, a Lonely Child who feels empty and lonely. In addition to the Self-aggrandizer and Lonely Child modes, we often note the presence of two other modes in these patients: the Detached Self-soother (a form of the avoidant maladaptive coping mode) and the Demanding Parent.

When narcissistic patients experience disappointments or other blows to their sensc of specialness, or when their feelings of loneliness come too close to the surface, they often use addictive or compulsive behaviors to soothe or calm these painful feelings (Detached Self-soother mode). For example, Brian, a stock-market "day trader," sought anonymous sex whenever his lonely feelings began to break through his successful façade. While these experiences provided a temporary respite, his feelings of loneliness remained or worsened.

At other times, narcissistic patients experience tremendous pressure to perform or achieve. They push themselves relentlessly to live up to their ideals of greatness or perfection. Anything less would mean failure, or even worse, mediocrity. This state of internal pressure is the Demanding Parent mode, an internalized parental voice that demands success or achievement at all costs.

The general goals in treating narcissistic patients with Schema Therapy are to heal the Lonely Child through limited reparenting, so that the patient's basic emotional needs are met; to empathically confront and set limits on the Self-aggrandizer so that the patient learns to view relationships in terms of equality and reciprocity, rather than entitlement and superiority; to help the patient learn to tolerate the pain of hurt and loneliness without escaping into self-soothing, compulsive, or addictive behaviors; and to confront the Demanding Parent so that the patient learns to value himself for his ordinary, human qualities, rather than only for his special abilities.

Making contact with the Lonely Child is the key to succeeding with narcissistic patients. Without this emotional "hook," narcissistic patients have little internal motivation to stick with therapy, although they may also be motivated by external considerations, such as keeping a marriage together or keeping a job. The extent to which narcissistic patients admit to having a lonely side varies, but we have been impressed by how many of these patients eventually acknowledge this side. For example,

Brian had amassed a small fortune by playing the stock market. His days were spent glued to his computer, where he made bets based on small fluctuations in the market. This obsessive activity kept him in a state of almost hypomanic excitement (i.e., Detached Self-soother mode), while confirming his sense of superiority as he consistently beat the odds (i.e., Self-aggrandizer mode). He spent most of the first session talking about his money, but broke down crying when the therapist asked if he had a lonely side, saying that no one had ever asked him that question.

One of the greatest challenges in working with narcissistic patients is seeing past their overcompensating modes to the Lonely Child within them. The therapist needs to remain empathic to the pain of the Lonely Child, while confronting the patient about the compensatory reasons for his arrogance and devaluation. This is not an easy process because the patient uses the same overcompensatory strategies to keep the therapist at a safe distance that he does with other people. He may question the therapist's qualifications, arrive late for sessions or cancel at the last minute, "forget" to pay his therapy bills, or roll his eyes in contempt when the therapist says something "stupid." Narcissistic patients can easily "push the therapist's buttons," especially if the therapist has schemas such as Defectiveness or Deprivation that are triggered by the patient's behavior. Narcissists tend to play interpersonal power games of the "top-dog, bottom-dog" variety (Campbell, Foster, & Finkel, 2002). These games reinforce their sense of superiority and enable them to avoid intimacy in relationships, which would leave them feeling exposed and vulnerable. To avoid getting caught up in these games the therapist needs to rise above them, rather than taking them personally.

In fact, in Schema Therapy with narcissists (as with other patients), the therapist uses the therapy relationship as a powerful vehicle for promoting change. The "here-and-now" interactions between patient and therapist offer the ideal opportunity to empathically confront the patient about his arrogant or devaluing behavior. This provides the patient with a vivid, palpable sense of his self-aggrandizing style, its effect on other people, and its overcompensatory purpose.

While theorizing on NPD has tended to emphasize the overcompensatory nature of this disorder, some authors (e.g., Fernando, 1998) have noted that spoiling a child represents a second, and possibly even more insidious, path towards NPD. Parents who spoil their children give them the message, either explicitly or implicitly, that they are entitled to "get what they want when they want it." Such children may grow up believing that others exist to serve their desires. They take their special status for granted and have little compunction about selfishly using or even exploiting other people. Thus, they have little or no regard for others' feelings, needs, or rights. Such individuals have difficulty tolerating limits or boundaries. They may become enraged when they are denied what they want. Such patients often have schemas that lie in the "Impaired Limits" domain, namely Entitlement and Insufficient Self-control/Self-discipline. They may be more difficult to treat than those with overcompensatory narcissism because they lack a Lonely Child mode that can be "hooked" into staying in treatment.

The key to working with "spoiled" narcissists is to empathically confront the Impulsive or Spoiled Child, the side of the patient that wants immediate gratification and finds it impossible to tolerate frustration. Schema dialogues with this side can be particularly effective. Therapists ask such patients to play the side that believes that "it is good to always get what you want when you want it." The therapist play the healthy side, challenging the patient's belief with contrary evidence. In essence, the therapist's argument is that, if you always get what you want you remain a child, unable to handle disappointments or frustrations, to pursue goals or plans, to get the rewards and privileges that come with being an adult. The therapists have to avoid the pitfall of framing their arguments in moral terms. Instead, they ask a pragmatic question: "Where has it gotten you to let a Spoiled Child run your life?"

In reality, many "spoiled" narcissists also experienced neglect, though they don't view it that way. Spoiling a child deprives him of the opportunity to grow, and sets him up for unrealistic expectations in the future, when he faces a world that is indifferent to his sense of entitlement. Moreover, many of these children were given everything that they wanted materially, while their emotional needs were ignored. Thus, educating the patient about the normal emotional needs of children may be the first step towards reparenting a narcissistic patient who has mistaken spoiling for love.

### *Treating antisocial personality disorder with Schema Therapy*

Many of the themes in working with narcissistic patients are also present in patients with antisocial personality disorder (ASPD). ASPD is defined in the DSM-IV (APA, 2000) by adult criminal behavior; an unstable, irresponsible, and reckless lifestyle; and a history of childhood conduct problems and delinquency. Psychopaths are the most severe subgroup of patients with antisocial personality disorder. In addition to criminal behavior and an antisocial lifestyle, these patients exhibit core psychopathic personality traits such as ruthlessness, remorselessness, callousness, and manipulation (Hare & Neumann, 2009). In essence, psychopaths use and exploit other people, lack empathy, and show little or no remorse for their actions. Many experts have assumed that psychopathic patients cannot be treated, and that psychotherapy may actually make such patients worse, by teaching them psychological skills that they would go on to use when conning or manipulating others. However, recent evidence is beginning to challenge this view (d'Silva, Duggan, & McCarthy, 2004).

Bernstein, Arntz, and De Vos (2007) have described several overcompensatory schema modes that are characteristic of antisocial and psychopathic patients. The Bully and Attack mode is a state in which patients use threats or aggression to assert their dominance, get something they want, or retaliate against a perceived threat or rival. When in this state, patients feel strong and powerful, compensating for underlying feelings of weakness and helplessness. In the Conning and Manipulative mode, patients use charm, lies, and manipulation to get something they want in an indirect manner. In the Paranoid Overcontroller mode, patients focus their attention on detecting a hidden threat or enemy. In the Predator mode, patients use cold, calculated aggression to eliminate a threat or rival. Bernstein and colleagues (2007) hypothesize that these four overcompensatory modes, together with the Self-aggrandizer mode, play a central role in violent and antisocial behavior.

A major randomized clinical trial of Schema Therapy for forensic patients with antisocial personality disorder and other Cluster B personality disorders is now taking place at seven forensic hospitals in The Netherlands. Although the study will not be completed for several years, early findings suggest that Schema Therapy is a promising treatment for forensic personality disorder patients, and especially for those with high levels of psychopathy (Bernstein, 2009).

27

## Specific points for working with couples

As an approach developed to treat long-standing emotional and relational issues, Schema Therapy offers a natural framework for understanding and addressing couples' distress. Many, if not most, problems that arise within close relationships can be understood through the prism of the partners' needs, schemas, coping styles, and modes, and through attending to the cycles of mutual triggering that often occur within relationships. Consequently, Schema Therapy assessment and intervention ideas offer a systematic way of addressing these current cycles, while linking them to the longer-standing life patterns of the couple and the individual partners. The ultimate goal of Schema Therapy for couples is parallel to the goal in individual therapy: alleviating distress and conflict by having each person's needs met. In the couples' context, recognizing and meeting both partners' needs is seen as a joint responsibility.

### *Applying the Schema Therapy model to couples*

As we discussed earlier, most maladaptive schemas involve an attempted adaptation to some relational shortfall, usually in the attachment bonds of early childhood. Extensive research in the past two decades has demonstrated that difficulties in attachment persist into adulthood, and exert a strong influence on a host of behaviors in the context of relationships (for a comprehensive recent review, see Mikulincer & Shaver, 2007). The basic developmental premises of Schema Therapy make the same point: that early relational deficits or problems will lead to future relational difficulties, with particular deficits or problems leading to corresponding unmet needs and to corresponding schemas. Indeed, the majority of the 18 schemas identified to date revolve around relational needs and manifest themselves very clearly in disturbed relational processes. For example, individuals with an Abandonment schema may be hypervigilant towards signs of rejection in their relationships; those with an Emotional Deprivation schema may feel that they are misunderstood or denied attention in both short- and long-term relationships; and ones with an Emotional Inhibition schema would refrain from any passionate or emotional displays, robbing themselves and their partners of any real gratification.

Similarly, most of the schema modes discussed earlier can appear in couples, often in ways that are mutually triggering. For example, a husband with an Emotional Inhibition schema may enter a Detached mode (which we may label the Overly Rational mode); his wife, who has an Emotional Deprivation schema, may feel shut out and flip into an Attention-seeking mode or a Demanding mode. Either of these will only deepen the husband's need to reign in any emotion, which in turn would exacerbate the wife's distress, and so on. These cycles can be understood, and defused, using Schema Therapy.

When working with couples or with individuals for whom romantic relationships are the key focus, we utilize the notion of "chemistry." Relationship researchers have yet to offer a full account of what constitutes chemistry (e.g., Eastwick, Finkel, Mochon, & Ariely, 2007; Fisher, 2004). Still, our clinical experience has taught us quite a few things about chemistry:

- It refers to the passionate, more than the companionate, component of love
- It can be very healthy for a relationship consisting of both physical and emotional attraction (which serve as a solid foundation for further relationship development)
- When feeling high chemistry, individuals tend to idealize their partners, and to see themselves as "destined" or "meant" for each other

- When chemistry is high, separation or absence tend to intensify one's feelings for the relationship partner; physical proximity leads to both emotional and sexual arousal.

Though chemistry is, to a certain degree, healthy and essential for engaging in any meaningful relationship, it can also underlie serious problems in relationships because it often arises from the activation of core schemas in one or both of the partners. This "schema chemistry" seems to characterize those instances where chemistry is very high (i.e., when initial attraction and idealization are extreme). Significantly, clients often enter relationships or choose to deepen them because of intense schema chemistry.

The typical triggers for schema chemistry are situations or people who lead a person to re-experience emotions that were familiar or situations that were emotionally charged in earlier life. This sense of familiarity (or of excitement) often keeps people in relationships that are unhealthy, or keeps them from attempting to improve the relationships for fear of changing these ineffable qualities. Several related problems can arise within relationships when schema chemistry is high. First, when partners mutually trigger each other's schemas, they almost invariably become incapable of truly meeting each other's needs: their distress is simply too high. Second, certain core schemas create oversensitivity to schema-related triggers, as well as cognitive biases (in attention, judgment, or memory) that distort the processing of everyday interactions – and therefore lead minor conflicts to escalate into much larger rifts. Third, and perhaps more importantly, other core schemas lead to insensitive or even abusive behaviors towards partners.

### *Conducting Schema Therapy with couples*

The goals of Schema Therapy for couples are to help partners meet each other's core needs by healing their schemas and reducing their destructive coping modes. In mode terms, the schema therapist teaches both partners to understand and access their own Child modes, and to enter either the Vulnerable Child or the Healthy Adult modes to de-escalate conflicts. The therapist also helps the partners learn to respond more sensitively (i.e., from a reparenting stance) to each other's Child modes. With time, the partners are taught to connect based on healthy chemistry instead of schema chemistry.

As is the case with Schema Therapy more generally, Schema Therapy for couples integrates ideas from CBT, Gestalt, and relational/attachment approaches to therapy. An assessment and education phase occurs first, followed by a change phase. Many assessment methods used in Schema Therapy for couples are similar to those used in individual Schema Therapy. However, much additional information becomes available to the therapist simply from observing the partners interact. Additionally, schema therapists often use one of the following:

(a) Imagery for assessment focused on the partner: The purpose of this exercise is to identify the schemas that are triggered in the relationship and to link them to unmet childhood needs.
(b) Detailed relationship histories: In these, each partner describes the development of their relationship over time. This helps identify both the strengths and the weaknesses of the relationship, and helps reveal the cycles of mutual triggering as it is experienced by both partners.

Once therapists have an understanding of the schemas and modes that are prominent in a couple's interactions, they convey this understanding back to the couple. This education can be aided by reviewing the Young Schema Questionnaires of both partners, or by assigning relevant chapters from *Reinventing your life* (Young & Klosko, 1993). More generally, the goal here is to link both current relational problems and longer-standing life patterns to the partners' schemas and modes and to the reciprocal processes to which they lead.

The change phase combines interpersonal, cognitive, emotional, and behavioral change strategies. Some of these are similar to techniques used in individual therapy while others are unique to the couples' context. The therapy employs both individual and conjoint sessions. Unlike earlier behavior therapy or CBT approaches, Schema Therapy focuses more on schema and mode changes and on conflict resolution within the couple than on simple skills training, communication, or problem-solving.

Conducting Schema Therapy with couples is a challenge. Therapists need to maintain a warm, genuine, and direct relationship with both partners, and to bond independently with each partner. They strive to maintain a balance of empathic confrontation: rather than maintaining neutrality, they make sure to side equally with the vulnerable and healthy modes of both partners, and to confront their maladaptive modes with relative balance. At the same time, they must ensure both partners' safety and contain the partners' conflict in the therapeutic room; this dictates responding forcefully to any abusive behavior by one or both of the partners. The ultimate (and difficult) goal is to model healthy reparenting among the partners without upstaging the partners themselves.

Early in the therapy, it is important to direct the couples towards emotional rather than practical issues. This avoids a common pitfall of couples' therapy, in which therapy simply becomes another venue in which the typical interactions (bickering, stonewalling, etc.) can take place. With this emotional (rather than practical) focus, the therapist may then use a variety of schema change techniques reviewed in earlier points. We will detail only some of them, to illustrate how they can be adapted to use with couples:

(a) Relationally: Therapists can teach partners how to attend to and meet each other's core needs – in other words, how to reparent each other.
(b) Cognitively: Both partners are taught to test the validity of their schemas, and to actively search for evidence

(particularly dis-confirming evidence that often goes unnoticed). They are then instructed to use schema flash-cards or diaries (see Point 21), both individually and together.

(c) Emotionally: One useful technique for increasing empathy between partners is to have each of them speak from the perspective of the Vulnerable Child, while encouraging the listener to imagine the speaker as that child – that is, to actively imagine their partner as the young and vulnerable child that he or she had been.

(d) Behaviorally: As in individual therapy, the behavioral pattern-breaking part often begins later in the therapy and lasts longest. Among the behavioral tools available for *couples* are the use of schema flashcards, focused on alternative adaptive dyadic behavior, and the use of role-plays and rehearsal to prepare for challenging situations that have previously led to escalating conflict or to distress.

Many sessions in the change phase revolve around understanding, and overcoming, schema clashes. When couples become more adept at doing this, attention can turn to predicting and preventing future conflicts. Ultimately, this leads to reduced distress. Nonetheless, when a relationship has been distressed for a long period, reducing the distress is often only half the work. The other half of the work is reintroducing positivity, playfulness, and fun. Therapists can approach this task as they would approach behavioral activation in the treatment of depression in an individual: instructing the partners to set aside regular times for one-on-one conversations and fun, working on improving affection and sexuality, and introducing rewarding and caring/loving positive gestures among the partners.

The schema therapist helps the couple evaluate realistically how much progress they have made, or could still make, in therapy. As couples' therapists of many orientations have noted, couples often enter therapy too late to salvage their relationship and a more realistic goal may be a trial separation. When that is the case, the schema therapist can have an important role in helping each of the partners prepare for future relationships with healthier schema choices and patterns. Both individual and conjoint sessions can be useful to help the partners understand and learn from what had happened in their relationship, and to help them resolve both practical and emotional issues that arise.

# 28

## Interplay between Schema Therapy for Axis II and CBT for Axis I

One benefit of utilizing Schema Therapy in clinical practice is that it can be integrated seamlessly with focused CBT interventions for Axis I disorders or symptoms. Such symptoms are often the presenting complaints with which patients enter therapy. When that is the case, the patient's acute symptomatic needs (e.g., a major depressive episode, panic disorder, or substance use) will guide the therapist to offer focused, evidence-based interventions. Even when the presenting complaints are longer-standing personality and relational problems, which lend themselves well to Schema Therapy, they are very commonly comorbid with specific Axis I diagnoses (including anxiety, mood, eating, substance use, and somatoform disorders), which lend themselves to narrower CBT protocols or other evidence-based approaches. It is therefore important to point out the interplay between Schema Therapy and CBT (or other evidence-based intervention approaches for Axis I problems).

Often, Axis I symptoms, severe as they are on their own, are embedded within a broader web of distress. In addition to the specific emotional or behavioral symptoms, the patient may have difficult or unsatisfying relationships, or be stuck in recurrent patterns of maladaptive behaviors and choices. This broader and more pervasive web is certainly characteristic of individuals with personality disorders, for whom Schema Therapy was originally developed. But it may be present for others as well; for example, some Axis I disorders (e.g., dysthymia or generalized anxiety disorder) can be understood well using the concepts of schemas, coping styles, and modes. And even among those for whom Axis I symptoms are primary, comorbid Axis II symptoms are very common.

Great strides have been made over the past few decades in the development of evidence-based treatment approaches for various Axis I disorders. Many of these treatments are time-limited and focused on particular disorders or sets of symptoms (e.g., exposure and response prevention for obsessive-compulsive disorder (Foa & Goldstein, 1978); behavioral activation for major depressive episodes (Jacobson, Martell, & Dimidjian, 2001); panic control therapy for panic disorder (Craske & Barlow, 2006)). Others adopt a broader, trans-diagnostic approach (Harvey, Watkins, Mansell, & Shafran, 2004; Roemer & Orsillo, 2008). A schema therapist can seamlessly implement any of these either before, or in concert with, the utilization of Schema Therapy.

This seamlessness is due, in part, to the fact that Schema Therapy began its way as an expansion of traditional CBT. Earlier in this book, we detailed how this expansion differentiates Schema Therapy from traditional CBT, but it is important to note that many of the guiding principles of Schema Therapy also make it compatible with other CBT interventions. First, like CBT, Schema Therapy advocates developing a collaborative case conceptualization (see Point 19). Case conceptualization is crucial for any effective therapy, and that is doubly true when patients present complex and challenging problems. Second, despite the longer time frame needed to carry out Schema Therapy, it too is a goal-driven therapy, and differs considerably from unstructured, often time-unlimited insight-oriented approaches. Third, Schema Therapy utilizes a variety of cognitive (Point 21) and behavioral (Point 23) techniques, and relies heavily on between-session "homework" or practice activities (though the nature of these may differ when the focus is on particular Axis I symptoms versus on schema change).

In practical terms, we recommend educating the patient early on about the different yet compatible natures of CBT and

Schema Therapy. In our center, we do this using a handout that is included in the intake packet, and which explains, in lay-person's terms, what CBT and Schema Therapy are. When creating our initial case conceptualization, we make sure that the patient fully understands which approach we plan to pursue and we note whether we recommend some combination of traditional CBT with Schema Therapy.

In some cases, Schema Therapy may precede the use of specific CBT interventions. For example, a patient who began therapy following a romantic breakup with the goal of understanding a life-long pattern of "bad relationship decisions" may slowly reveal the presence of specific mood, anxiety, or other symptoms, ones that are amenable to particular evidence-based interventions. Having presented Schema Therapy as an extension of CBT, focused on different goals but sharing the same underlying principles, such a shift would not feel like an abrupt about-face. Therefore, a schema therapist could, relatively easily, recommend revisiting the priorities of the therapy (i.e., the topics to discuss in-session, or the intervention techniques to use) when appropriate.

In other cases, therapy begins with CBT and transitions into Schema Therapy. Many patients who benefit from time-limited interventions come to the realization that they would like to broaden the scope of their experience in therapy. After all, a successful course of CBT often brings to the surface broader and more long-standing issues that go beyond the specific symptoms addressed. Simultaneously, it also tends to create strong rapport between the patient and the therapist. The familiarity, warmth, and trust that grow out of a validating and empowering therapeutic experience can serve as a solid foundation for the longer (and often more difficult) process of schema change. It is an opportunity that is often squandered when traditional CBT therapists do not feel "qualified" to be working on therapeutic goals that seem more psychodynamic in nature. The integrative nature of Schema Therapy, the balance it strikes between supportiveness and goal-setting, and its compatibility with CBT mean that it builds a bridge between short-term interventions and longer-term therapy. Obviously, not every patient in CBT must cross this bridge; however, its availability is welcomed by many patients and therapists.

# 29

## The therapeutic relationship: Limited reparenting

As we explained earlier (Point 14), limited reparenting is the bounded fulfillment of the patient's needs by a flexible and genuine therapist. Below, we expand on the clinical practicalities of the limited reparenting therapeutic stance.

First, it is essential to recognize that limited reparenting takes on many forms. Of course warmth, genuineness, and empathy, the "non-specific" factors that underlie most effective therapy and that were clearly articulated by Carl Rogers (1951), characterize the work of schema therapists in any interaction with patients. Nonetheless, the manner in which a schema therapist goes beyond these basic characteristics and delivers limited reparenting will differ considerably from patient to patient based on the patient's unmet needs. The manner may also differ within a single therapeutic relationship based on the predominant modes that are active at any session or moment. Thus, an early step in the assessment and education phase of every course of therapy is to determine what style of limited reparenting is most appropriate for the particular patient.

At times, the patient's needs become quickly evident. For example, a patient with a strong Emotional Deprivation schema may score high on the relevant items on the Young Schema Questionnaire and the Young Parenting Inventory, and may readily provide examples from current life circumstances in which they feel invalidated or deprived of attention. The importance of warmth and validation in the therapist's repertoire would thus be very clear.

At other times, needs may be less evident, certainly to the patients themselves. For example, a patient with a Defectiveness schema, but with a predominant coping style of overcompensation, may enter therapy with an air of invulnerability, and possibly with a superior and dismissive attitude. The therapist's role is to recognize these as coping behaviors, but also to identify the core vulnerability and the unmet need to which they are tied, and to respond to them as a good parent would. In this case (which occurs often in the treatment of patients with narcissistic features; see Point 26), the key to good limited reparenting would be to nurture and understand the Vulnerable Child, while placing limits on the distancing, dismissive behaviors of the Self-aggrandizer.

This last example speaks to one of the most important features of limited reparenting (and of parenting itself): the need for flexibility. Just as the needs of one child may differ from those of another, the needs of one patient may diverge from those of the next. Therapists need to adjust their style to fit the needs of the patient – which may vary from session to session or even within a session. Serving as a model for the patient's own emerging Healthy Adult mode, the therapist needs to be able to provide any of the following: stability and a basis for secure attachment; scaffolding for autonomy and competence; encouragement for the discovery and expression of genuine needs and emotions; appreciation of spontaneity and play (and aid in reducing inhibitions for these); and finally, honesty and directness about realistic limits both within the therapy itself and outside of it.

There are specific reparenting goals that are tailored for particular needs or schemas. For example, in treating patients with Mistrust/Abuse schemas, schema therapists place greatest importance on transparency and honesty with the patient. They explicitly discuss trust and intimacy topics, and they demonstrate trustworthiness (e.g., by answering questions immediately and directly, rather than first exploring their meaning). They encourage the patient to voice any negative feelings they may have toward the therapist, and they proceed with great caution when suggesting more emotionally activating interventions (such as imagery), thus validating the patient's vulnerability.

A different set of goals is pursued in treating patients with, say, Entitlement schemas. In such cases, the main goal is to get beyond the entitlement to the underlying vulnerability. This vulnerability is nurtured, while the entitled side is not reinforced. As part of the reparenting, the therapist empathically confronts the entitlement and places limits on it. More importantly, rather than engaging in a struggle for power or control with the patient, the therapist emphasizes emotional connection. Similar tailored goals exist for each of the schemas but listing them would be beyond the scope of this Point. For more details, see Young et al. (2003).

Limited reparenting is not a strategy in its own right. Instead, it is a guiding therapeutic stance – a broad approach to the therapist's role – one that is integrated with the therapeutic interventions (cognitive, experiential, behavioral) that are used. Indeed, much of the experiential work done in Schema Therapy involves reparenting. When a therapist enters a patient's image and responds as a Healthy Adult, the therapist is reparenting the patient. Demonstrating healthy responses to the patient's needs, or even allowing the patient to acknowledge those needs, teaches the patient that there are other ways a parent might have responded to them – and ultimately, that there are other ways that their own Healthy Adult could reparent themselves.

To summarize, limited reparenting does not involve the therapist actually becoming a parent or regressing the patient into childlike dependency. Instead, it works within ethical and professional boundaries to approximate the patient's missed, and needed, emotional experiences. Using this approximation, it strives to provide for the patient's unmet needs and to heal the patient's maladaptive schemas.

Limited reparenting is impossible without considerable emotional investment on the therapist's part. Being genuine, and conveying this genuineness in their tone of voice, their words, and their actions means that schema therapists allow themselves to be real people, not detached clinicians, in the therapy relationship. As a consequence, delivering limited reparenting successfully is often quite challenging, as the degree of both skill and empathy required is high. To meet this challenge well, therapists must be well acquainted with their own schemas and coping styles (see Point 30), to help them remain focused on reparenting the patient.

# 30

## Therapists' own schemas

Like the patients they treat, therapists often have early maladaptive schemas based on their own painful life experiences. Healing one's own schemas is excellent preparation for helping others. However, to the extent that these schemas remain unresolved, therapists can remain vulnerable to schema activation. This is, in fact, almost inevitable, as schema healing is rarely complete. At times of unusual stress, or when confronted with patients that "push our buttons," one's schemas can become triggered. Usually, therapists have a Healthy Adult mode, aware of their own schemas, that can take corrective action when these schemas threaten to interfere with the treatment being given. In certain circumstances or with certain patients, however, this schema activation may cause more serious problems, especially when it is combined with unhealthy forms of coping.

One sure sign that a therapist's schemas and coping responses are interfering with therapy is boundary transgressions: either the therapist allows the patient to transgress his or her boundaries, or the therapist transgresses the patient's boundaries. An example of the former involves therapists who allow patients to make excessive demands on them, or to treat them disrespectfully or abusively. Self-sacrifice, Unrelenting Standards, and Approval-seeking are among the most common schemas seen in therapists. Therapists often come from families where they learned to be highly attuned to the needs and feelings of others, and played the role of caregiver with other family members, such as parents or siblings. These experiences can be a source of positive motivation for providing therapy. However, they can also leave therapists vulnerable to certain pitfalls, such as being too focused on their patients' needs at the expense of their own (Self-sacrifice schema); being too hard on themselves or their patients (Unrelenting Standards schema); or being too dependent on their patients' approval as a source of self-worth (Approval-seeking schema).

Some therapists may give their patients too much of their time or attention. For example, one therapist allowed Julie, a patient with borderline personality disorder, to send him daily, lengthy emails, which he felt compelled to answer, even when he was very busy. Julie found this daily attention very satisfying, but the therapist eventually found it to be too much. The therapist's own mother had borderline personality disorder. As a child, he had been his mother's emotional caregiver, ignoring his own needs and feelings to take care of his mother's. Because of his Self-sacrifice schema, he responded to his patient's demands by giving her yet more of his time. He didn't realize the toll it was taking on him until things had gone too far. Only after receiving supervision on the case was he able to set limits on Julie's emailing, leading to a successful resolution.

The therapist's schema modes can also contribute to patients' boundary transgressions. For example, some therapists respond to their patients' anger, aggression, or devaluation by becoming too solicitous or subservient (Compliant Surrenderer mode). The more bullying, demeaning, or angry the patient becomes, the "nicer," more soft-spoken, and more compliant the therapist becomes. One therapist had a patient, Ron, who spent his sessions in sullen silence. Ron stared at the floor and responded to the therapist's questions with one-word answers. He radiated hostility, which he expressed through his silent refusal to engage in the treatment. The therapist was a soft-spoken, gentle woman who had difficulty acknowledging her own anger. She had been taught to be a "good girl," who didn't talk back and who attempted to please others (Compliant Surrenderer mode). In response to Ron's silences, the therapist persisted in attempting to engage him. She searched for topics to introduce in the session and was unfailingly polite and friendly. Inside, she felt more worthless and incompetent with each passing session. One day, 6 months into the therapy, she broke down crying in her supervision session, saying that she couldn't take it anymore. The supervisor recommended that she confront Ron, and set limits on his hostile, withholding behavior. In the next session, she did so successfully, an intervention that represented a turning point in the therapy, and in the therapist's own personal and professional development.

Another possible pitfall for schema therapists is that their focus on needs and on reparenting may trigger their own unmet needs; these may then get acted out with the patient. For example, a therapist with a strong Emotional Deprivation schema may seek the love that he was lacking as a child in his relationship with his patients. The therapist may have a fantasy of perfect love, which he, as therapist, vicariously experiences by trying to become the all-giving, all-loving parent to his patients. Unfortunately, such situations run the risk of going awry and leading to boundary transgressions, as when a therapist becomes romantically involved with his patient. Such cases almost always involve strong schema activation in the therapist.

While persistent boundary violations are one sign that the therapist's schemas have been triggered, disengagement from the patient can be another. Therapists with an Emotional Inhibition schema, for example, may become uncomfortable with their patients' emotionality. For example, they may subtly, though unconsciously, discourage their patients from showing emotions, by becoming critical (Punitive Parent mode) or overly intellectualized (Detached Protector mode) when their patients become emotional. When both therapist and patient share this discomfort, the result can be an unwitting "conspiracy" to avoid emotions altogether. The therapist and patient engage in intellectual discussions so that they can avoid the discomfort they both feel with more emotional or intimate topics. Their Detached Protector modes mutually reinforce each other. They may talk about the patient's schemas but they would do so in a detached manner that ultimately fails to produce change.

Similarly, therapists with a strong Emotional Deprivation schema may be threatened by intimacy, which triggers their own unmet needs. They may become distant and detached in the face of the patient's need for closeness, a withdrawal that may parallel the childhood origins of their own emotional deprivation.

In dealing with more challenging patients, such as those with borderline, narcissistic, or antisocial personality disorder, even experienced therapists should ensure that they have adequate support. Supervision, peer supervision, and the therapist's own therapy can help avoid pitfalls or get the therapy back on track when the therapist's own schemas get triggered. We strongly believe that good schema therapists should be mindful of the support that they need and deserve so they can conduct this complex and nuanced therapy in a way that is effective for their patients, and fulfilling for themselves.

# References

Alexander, F., & French, T. M. (1946). *Psychoanalytic therapy: Principles and application*. Oxford, England: Ronald Press.

American Psychiatric Association (2000). *Diagnostic and statistical manual of mental disorders* (4th ed., text revision). Washington, DC: American Psychiatric Association.

Arntz, A., & van Genderen, H. (2009). *Schema therapy for borderline personality disorder*. Chichester, England: John Wiley & Sons Ltd.

Bartlett, F. C. (1932). *Remembering: An experimental and social study*. New York: Cambridge University Press.

Bateman, A. W., & Fonagy, P. (2004). Mentalization-based Treatment of BPD. *Journal of Personality Disorders, 18*, 36–51.

Baumeister, R. F., & Leary, M. R. (1995). The need to belong: Desire for interpersonal attachments as a fundamental human motivation. *Psychological Bulletin, 117*, 497–529.

Beck, A. T. (1972). *Depression: Causes and treatment*. Philadelphia, PA: University of Pennsylvania Press.

Beck, A. T., Freeman, A., & Davis, D. D. (2003). *Cognitive therapy of personality disorders*. New York: Guilford Press.

Bernstein, D. (2009, December 11). Treating the untreatable: Schema Focused Therapy for high scoring psychopaths. Paper Presentation, Trent Study Day, Nottingham, England, UK.

Bernstein, D. P., Arntz, A., & de Vos, M. (2007). Schema focused therapy in forensic settings: Theoretical model and recommendations for best clinical practice. *International Journal of Forensic Mental Health*, *6*, 169–183.

Borkovec, T. D., Alcaine, O. M., & Behar, E. (2004). Avoidance theory of worry and generalized anxiety disorder. In R. G. Heimberg, C. L. Turk, & D. S. Mennin (Eds.), *Generalized anxiety disorders: Advances in research and practice* (pp. 77–108). New York: Guilford Press.

Brewin, C. R., Andrews, B., & Gotlib, I. H. (1993). Psychopathology and early experience: A reappraisal of retrospective reports. *Psychological Bulletin*, *113*, 82–98.

Butler, A. C., Brown, G. K., Beck, A. T., & Grisham, J. R. (2002). Assessment of dysfunctional beliefs in borderline personality disorder. *Behaviour Research and Therapy*, *40*, 1231–1240.

Campbell, W. K., Foster, C., & Finkel, E. (2002). Does self-love lead to love for others? A story of narcissistic game playing. *Journal of Personality and Social Psychology*, *83*, 340–354.

Clarkin, J. F., Yeomans, F. E., & Kernberg, O. F. (1999). *Psychotherapy for borderline personality*. Hoboken, NJ: John Wiley & Sons Ltd.

Craske, M. G., & Barlow, D. H. (2006). *Mastery of your panic and anxiety: Therapist guide* (3rd ed.). New York: Oxford University Press.

David, D., & Szentagotai, A. (2006). Cognitions in cognitive-behavioral psychotherapies: Towards an integrative model. *Clinical Psychology Review*, *26*, 284–298.

Davidson, P. R., & Parker, K. C. H. (2001). Eye movement desensitization and reprocessing (EMDR): A meta-analysis. *Journal of Consulting and Clinical Psychology*, *69*, 305–316.

Deci, E. L., & Ryan, R. M. (2000). The "what" and "why" of goal pursuits: Human needs and the self-determination of behavior. *Psychological Inquiry*, *11*, 227–268.

d'Silva, K., Duggan, C., & McCarthy, L. (2004). Does treatment really make psychopaths worse? A review of the evidence. *Journal of Personality Disorders*, *18*, 163–177.

Eastwick, P. W., Finkel, E. J., Mochon, D., & Ariely, D. (2007). Selective versus unselective romantic desire. *Psychological Science*, *18*, 317–319.

Eysenck, H. J. (1990). Biological dimensions of personality. In L. A. Previn (Ed.), *Handbook of personality: Theory and research* (pp. 244–276). New York: Guilford Press.

Farrell, J. M., Shaw, I. A., & Webber, M. A. (2009). A schema-focused approach to group psychotherapy for outpatients with borderline personality disorder: A randomized controlled trial. *Journal of Behavior Therapy and Experimental Psychiatry*, *40*, 317–328.

Fernando, J. (1998). The etiology of narcissistic personality disorder. *The Psychoanalytic Study of the Child*, *53*, 141–158.

Fisher, H. (2004). *Why we love: The nature and chemistry of romantic love*. New York: Henry Holt.

Foa, E. B., & Goldstein, A. (1978). Continuous exposure and complete response prevention in the treatment of obsessive-compulsive neurosis. *Behavior Therapy*, *9*, 821–829.

Foa, E., Hembree, E., Cahill, S., Rauch, A., Riggs, D., Feeny, N., & Yadin, E. (2005). Randomized trial of prolonged exposure for posttraumatic stress disorder with and without cognitive restructuring: Outcome at academic and community clinics. *Journal of Consulting and Clinical Psychology*, *73*, 953–964.

Foa, E., Hembree, E., & Rothbaum, B. O. (2007). *Prolonged exposure therapy for PTSD: Emotional reprocessing of traumatic experiences, therapist guide*. New York: Oxford University Press.

Freud, S. (1924). *Collected papers*. New York: International Psychoanalytic Press.

Giesen-Bloo, J., Van Dyck, R., Spinhoven, P., Van Tilburg, W., Dirksen, C., Van Asselt, et al. (2006). Outpatient psychotherapy for borderline personality disorder: A randomized trial of schema-focused therapy vs. transference-focused psychotherapy. *Archives of General Psychiatry*, *63*, 649–658.

Glasser, W. (1969). *Reality therapy*. New York: Harper & Row.

Gray, J. A. (1990). Brain systems that mediate both emotion and cognition. *Cognition and Emotion*, *4*, 269–288.

Hare, R. D., & Neumann, C. S. (2009). Psychopathy. In P. H. Blaney & T. Millon (Eds.), *Oxford textbook of psychopathology, second edition* (pp. 622–650). New York: Oxford University Press.

Harvey, A. G., Watkins, E., Mansell, W., & Shafran, R. (2004). *Cognitive behavioural processes across psychological disorders: A transdiagnostic approach to research and treatment*. New York: Oxford University Press.

Horney, K. (1946). *Our inner conflicts*. London: Routledge and Kegan Paul.

Jacobson, N. S., Martell, C. R., & Dimidjian, S. (2001). Behavioral activation treatment for depression: Returning to contextual roots. *Clinical Psychology: Science and Practice*, *8*, 255–270.

Kellogg, S. (2004). Dialogical encounters: Contemporary perspectives on “chairwork” in psychotherapy. *Psychotherapy: Theory, Research, Practice, Training*, *41*, 310–320.

Kernberg, O. (1976). Technical considerations in the treatment of borderline personality organization. *Journal of the American Psychoanalytic Association*, *24*, 795–829.

Khantzian, E. J. (1997). The self-medication hypothesis of substance use disorders: A reconsideration and recent applications. *Harvard Review of Psychiatry*, *4*, 231–244.

Lazarus, A. A., & Lazarus, C. N. (1991). Multimodal Life History Inventory. Champaign, IL: Research Press.

Linehan, M. M. (1993). *Cognitive-behavioral treatment of borderline personality disorder*. New York: Guilford Press.

Loewald, H. (1980). *Repetition and repetition compulsion. Papers on Psychoanalysis*. New Haven, CT: Yale Press.

Maslow, A. (1962). *Toward a psychology of being*. New York: Van Nostrand.

Mikulincer, M., & Shaver, P. R. (2007). *Attachment in adulthood: Structure, dynamics, and change*. New York: Guilford Press.

Nordahl, H. M., & Nysaeter, T. E. (2005). Schema therapy for patients with borderline personality disorder: A single case series. *Journal of Behavior Therapy and Experimental Psychiatry*, *36*, 254–264.

Padesky, C. A. (1994). Schema change processes in cognitive therapy. *Clinical Psychology and Psychotherapy*, *1*, 267–278.

Persons, J. B. (2008). *The case formulation approach to cognitive-behavior therapy*. New York: Guilford Press.

Piaget, J. (1955). *The child's construction of reality*. London: Routledge and Kegan Paul.

Roemer, L., & Orsillo, S. M. (2008). *Mindfullness and acceptance based behavioral therapies in practice*. New York: Guilford Press.

Rogers, C. R. (1951). *Client-centered therapy: Its current practice, implications, and theory*. Oxford, England: Houghton Mifflin.

Ronningstam, E. (2009). Narcissistic personality disorder. In P. H. Blaney & T. Millon (Eds.), *Oxford textbook of psychopathology, second edition* (pp. 752–771). New York: Oxford University Press.

Safran, J. D., & Muran, J. C. (1996). The resolution of ruptures in the therapeutic alliance. *Journal of Consulting and Clinical Psychology*, *64*, 447–458.

Segal, Z., & Shaw, B. (1996). Cognitive therapy. *American Psychiatric Press Review of Psychiatry*, *15*, 69–90.

Skinner, B. F. (1953). *Science and human behavior*. New York: Macmillan.

Smucker, M. R., & Boos, A. (2005). Imagery rescripting and reprocessing therapy. In A. Freeman, M. Stone, & D. Martin (Eds.), *Comparative treatments for borderline personality disorder* (pp. 215–237). New York: Springer Publishing Co.

Uhlmann, E., Pizarro, D., & Bloom, P. (2008). Varieties of social cognition. *Journal for the Theory of Social Behavior*, *38*, 293–322.

Wachtel, P. L. (2007). *Relational theory and the practice of psychotherapy*. New York: Guilford Press.

Young, J. E. (1990). *Cognitive therapy for personality disorders: A schema-focused approach*. Sarasota, FL: Professional Resource Exchange, Inc.

Young, J. E., & Flanagan, C. (1998). Schema-focused therapy for narcissistic patients. In E. Ronningstam (Ed.), *Disorders of narcissism: Diagnostic, clinical, and empirical implications* (pp. 239–268). Washington, DC: American Psychiatric Press.

Young, J. E., & Klosko, J. S. (1993). *Reinventing your life*. New York: Dutton.

Young, J. E., Klosko, J. S., & Weishaar, M. E. (2003). *Schema therapy: A practitioner's guide*. New York: Guilford Press.

# Index